Ancient Peoples and Places

EARLY BUDDHIST JAPAN

General Editor

DR. GLYN DANIEL

To My Parents

ABOUT THE AUTHOR

Dr Kidder has had long residence in China, Korea and Japan, and travelled widely in Europe and the Far East. He received his M.A. and Ph.D. degrees from New York University and taught at Washington University in St Louis before going to International Christian University in Tokyo in 1956. He is Professor of Art History and Archaeology at I.C.U. and was chairman of the Humanities Division from 1966 to 1970. He was a Visiting Lecturer at Yale University in 1964–65 and Visiting Professor of Oriental Art at the University of Oregon in 1971.

He has participated in excavations in Japan at different times since 1950 and has conducted excavations on the large Neolithic and Palaeolithic community site on the grounds of I.C.U. since 1957. He is the author of many articles and reviews, and several books, including The Jōmon Pottery of Japan *(1957),* Japan before Buddhism *(1959, revised 1966),* Masterpieces of Japanese Sculpture *(1961),* Japanese Temples *(1964),* The Birth of Japanese Art *(1964),* Early Japanese Art *(1965), and* Prehistoric Japanese Arts: Jōmon Pottery *(1968).*

EARLY BUDDHIST JAPAN

J. Edward Kidder

90 PHOTOGRAPHS
61 LINE DRAWINGS
6 MAPS
1 TABLE

PRAEGER PUBLISHERS
New York · Washington

THIS IS VOLUME SEVENTY-EIGHT IN THE SERIES
Ancient Peoples and Places
GENERAL EDITOR: DR. GLYN DANIEL

BOOKS THAT MATTER

*Published in the United States of America in 1972
by Praeger Publishers Inc., 111 Fourth Avenue,
New York, N.Y. 10003*

*First published in Great Britain in 1972 by
Thames and Hudson Ltd, London*

Library of Congress Catalog Card Number: 70-189060

Printed in Great Britain

CONTENTS

List of Illustrations

PLATES

FIGURES

Abbreviations used in line drawings

(Hyphenations are included to indicate the break down of the words)

Temples
B Belfry (Shō-rō)
c Cloister (Kai-rō)
D Dormitory (Sō-bō)
EMH East Main Hall (Golden Hall) (Tō-kon-dō)
ER East Rooms (Tō-shitsu)
K Kitchen (Sui-den)
LH Lecture Hall (Kō-dō)
MG Middle Gate (Chū-mon)
MH Main Hall (Golden Hall) (Kon-dō)
MMH Middle Main Hall (Golden Hall) (Chū-kon-dō)
NCH North Circular Hall (Hoku-en-dō)
NG North Gate (Hoku-mon)
P Pagoda (Tō)
p Pantry (Sei-den)
R Refectory (Jiki-dō)
SD Small Dormitory (Shō-shi-bō)
SG South Gate (Nan-mon)

SGG South Great Gate (Nan-dai-mon)
SR Sūtra Repository (Kyō-zō)
WMH West Main Hall (Golden Hall) (Sai-kon-dō)
WR West Rooms (Sai-shitsu)

Palaces
AP Administration Palace (Chō-dō-in)
IAH Imperial Assembly Hall (Chō-shū-den)
ICH Imperial Council Hall (Hall of State) (Dai-goku-den)
IR Imperial Residence (Dai-ri)

garan—cloister-surrounded nucleus of a temple
gū, miya—palace, shrine
ji, dera—temple
jō—castle
kyō—capital

Ruler's Number	Posthumous Name	Reign Dates AD	Name of Palace	Location of Palace[4]
29	Kimmei	539–571	Shikishima no Kunasashi	Kanaya, Sakurai city
30	Bidatsu	572–585	Kudara-ōi	Kudara, Koryō-chō
31	Yōmei	585–587	Ikebe-namitsuki	Abe, Sakurai city
32	Sushun	587–592	Kurahashi no Shibagaki	Kurahashi, Sakurai city
33	Suiko (F)	592–628	Toyura	Asuka village
			Owarida	„ „
34	Jomei	628–641	Asuka Okamoto	Kudara, Koryō-chō
			Kudara	„ „
			Tanaka	Tanaka, Kashiwara city
			Umasaka	Mise, Kashiwara city
35	Kōgyoku (F)	641–645 a	Asuka Itabuki	Oka, Asuka village
			Naniwa no Nagara Toyasaki	Osaka city
36	Kōtoku	645–654	„ „ „ „	„ „
37	Saimei[1] (F)	655–661	„ „ „ „	„ „
			Asuka Kawahara	Kawahara, Asuka village
			Nochino Asuka Okamoto	Oka, Asuka village
38	Tenchi	661–671	Ōmi or Ōtsu	Ōtsu city, Shiga prefecture
39	Kōbun	672	„ „ „	„ „ „ „
40	Temmu	672–686	Asuka Kiyomigahara; Naniwa	Asuka, Asuka village
41	Jitō (F)	686–697 a	Fujiwara	Takadono, Kashiwara city
42	Mommu	697–707	„	„ „ „
43	Gemmyō (F)	707–715 a	„	„ „ „
			Heijō	Saki-chō, Nara city
44	Genshō (F)	715–724 a	„	„ „ „
45	Shōmu	724–749 a	Heijō; Kuni; Naniwa; Shigaraki	„ „ „
46	Kōken (F)	749–758 a	„	„ „ „
47	Junnin	758–764 a[2]	„ Hora	„ „ „
48	Shōtoku[3] (F)	764–770	„ Yuge	„ „ „
49	Kōnin	770–781	„	„ „ „
50	Kammu	781–806	„	„ „ „
			Nagaoka	Nagaoka-chō, Otokuni county, Kyoto prefecture
			Heian	Kyoto city

(F): Empress   a: Abdicated   [1] Same person as Kōgyoku   [2] Forced off the throne
[3] Same person as Kōken   [4] In Nara prefecture unless otherwise indicated

Name of Tomb⁵	Location of Tomb by prefecture	KEYHOLE	SQUARE	ROUND	Co-burial	Cremation
Hinokuma no Sakaai	Nara	x			x	
Kawachi no Shinaga no Nakaai	Osaka	x			x	
Kawachi no Shinaga no Hara	,,		x			
Kurahashi no Okanoe	Nara			x		
Shinaga no Yamada	Osaka		x		x	
Osaka no Uchi	Nara		x⁶	x	x	
Osaka no Shinaga	Osaka			x		
Ochi no Okanoe	Nara			x	x	
Yamashina	Kyoto		x⁶	x		
Nagara no Yamazaki	Shiga			x		
Hinokuma Ōuchi	Nara			x⁷	x	
Hinokuma Ōuchi	,,			x⁷	x	x
Hinokuma no Ako	,,					x
Nahoyama no Higashi	,,					x
Nahoyama no Nishi	,,					x
Sahoyama no Minami	,,					
Awaji	Osaka (Awaji Is.)					
Takanu	Nara					
Tawara no Higashi	,,			x		
Kashiwabara	,,			x		

⁵ All imperial tombs are called *misasagi* or *ryō* (mausoleum) whether mounded or not
⁶ Round mound on square base ⁷ More or less octagonal

Preface

A book that deals essentially with the archaeology of the early centuries of Buddhism in Japan is not going to be an exception to the common problems of arriving at acceptable forms for Japanese words and ideas for which there are no English equivalents. Time after time the awkward-ness of the situation is exemplified.

Anything resembling total consistency is far too much to expect in a translation into English of names for buildings and ranks, not to mention numerous objects. Some names of buildings do have adequate English equivalents (*i.e.* South Gate) or are known by popular English terms (*i.e.* pagoda). Whether accurate or not, by custom or logic, these are usually regarded as satisfactory. Many others are far less so, but an effort has been made to translate as many as can be reasonably done. A key is provided on p. 9 for the letters marking the buildings in the figures illustrating ground plans of palaces and temples. The inconsistency in omitting macrons from well known place and other names (*i.e.* Tokyo, Kyoto, Osaka, Shinto, etc.) simply falls in line with current practice.

I have followed Japanese procedure in using the old names for Nara and Kyoto, that is to say, Heijō and Heian. The former is the eighth-century city under excavation today, to the west of the modern city of Nara. The name of Heian was changed when another capital was established in modern times.

The relatively recent redistricting of administrative areas for cities (*shi*) and smaller units has resulted in some instances in the assignment to city governments of immense territory lying well outside the densely popu-lated areas. Since one's customary experience in medium to small-sized cities is with city limits located near the outer edges of the heavily populated areas, it has sometimes come as a surprise to find a site listed as within a city yet to be, in fact, far out in open country. When I have known this to be the case, I have indicated it by adding the words 'jurisdictional area' to the location of a site in the captions.

I am indebted to a number of people for their kindness in supplying photographs for this book. Many came from Nagano Rokumeisō in Nara city. I wish to express my appreciation to them and to the following individuals and, in some cases, the agencies with which they are connected: Mr Taku Tanaka, Nara Cultural Properties Committee responsible for the Heijō site; Mr Takashi Sōma of the National Museum, Tokyo; Mr Hiroshi Kitazawa, photographer of the aerial view of the Funada site; Mr Kōichi Shirakawa and Mr Ryūdō Habara for pictures of roof tiles from Kagawa prefecture; the Nachi Shrine office; and the Fukuoka prefectural office for the view of the excavation of Dazaifu. Mr Akifumi Oikawa took time out to photograph fortifications in Kyushu for me. My assistant, Mr Shūzō Koyama, has been of constant aid and a vast reservoir of knowledge. I owe him a special word of thanks. My wife has made many suggestions concerning the manuscript. Her encouragement and patience wore well throughout the long delays in finishing the manuscript.

J.E.K.

CHAPTER I

Early Japanese History

From the Japanese view-point of Japanese history, the conventional historical concepts were in shambles at the end of the second World War. The Japanese defeat undermined the accepted beliefs in the divinity of the emperor and in the 'history' of the country's origins. From that time, all restrictions to thought having been removed, historians have been energetically reclassifying 'facts' as fancy, rearranging old data, opening up new areas of investigation, and expanding political and social theories.

Needless to say, all other forms of intellectual endeavour have ben-efited, not the least of which is archaeology. It may not be too much to say that, despite the unshackling of the historian and therefore his elevation to neo-pioneer status for at least early Japanese history, the most new knowledge of the period has been accumulated through archae-ological work. A primary aim here is to utilize this surprisingly large quantity of material in trying to trace the development of the monuments and their furnishings, the application of the laws, and the historical events about which the old texts are vague or silent. And art historical changes may be better understood by making use of the dates suggested through archaeological investigations.

The archaeology of historic periods is a late-comer to the archaeological scene in Japan. Abandoned temple sites had occasionally been dug in the 1920's, but not until fairly recently was it realized how much information such sites could yield, and that none exists in a vacuum: the more sites dug, the easier it becomes to understand similar sites. Historic excavations are not always spectacular and frequently do not produce aesthetically attractive objects for museum displays, but they have invariably been informative.

Some preoccupation with ground plans may be excused because in so many cases only foundation stones remain. The refinements of archaeology make one able to reconstruct the general appearance of the nucleus of a temple if only a few base stones are in place for the wooden columns of some of the buildings. This, however, would not be possible were it not for the fact that a sampling of buildings is preserved from each period; these buildings furnish the ingredients for the formulae required in architectural reconstruction.

This stage in Japanese history is characterized by a familiar three-way relationship between the emperor, the aristocracy and the clergy. Ranging between balance, alliances and open feuds, the condition was compounded by an also not unfamiliar pro-foreign and an anti-foreign rivalry between the leading families, much of which depended on their ancestry and vested interests.

INTRODUCTION OF BUDDHISM

The period starts with the first officially recorded contact in AD 552 between Buddhism and the Japanese court. According to the *Nihon Shoki*, the Chronicles of Japan, an eighth century compilation that terminates in the year 697, Emperor Kimmei, who is officially listed as the twenty-ninth ruler of Japan, received some gifts from the king of Paekche, a country in south-west Korea. These Buddhist articles accompanied a request for more aid against Silla, the kingdom in the south-east part of the peninsula. This incident was by no means the first contact with Korean culture. There is ample evidence of contact many hundreds of years earlier, but it is a workable starting point for the introduction of sophisticated cultural ideas to Japan. Doubtless there were practising Buddhist immigrants already in Japan, and the *Shoku Nihongi*, another old text which covers the years 697–792 but is considered to be somewhat less reliable, implies that the official introduction was in 538. Either way, the presence of Buddhists in Japan had negligible effect until the emperors themselves took a serious interest in it. Yōmei (31) was said to have been converted to Buddhism, but it is not certain whether his successor, Sushun (32), was a Buddhist or not. These emperors were designated 31 and 32 in the official numbering of Japanese rulers (see the list of emperors on pp. 10, 11). Sushun resided on the outskirts of territory controlled by the Soga, the strongest clan favouring Buddhism, and seemed to have been engineering the assassination of Soga no Umako before the tables were turned on him in one of the rare murders of a Japanese ruler.

With the death of Sushun, the anti-Buddhist Mononobe family lost much influence, and the appearance of Empress Suiko (33) on the scene, with her Soga connections, paved the way for the rapid development of Buddhism, sponsored by Prince Shōtoku, whom she appointed as regent and heir apparent. The palace was situated in more solid Soga territory, in the heart of the Asuka region, which was soon built up as a hard-core Buddhist centre. Among the leading families, and those in the contest that decided the future of Buddhism, the Nakatomi were south-east of the Asuka region, the Mononobe well to the north-east, and the Otomo to the south-west. There were others, but of less importance.

Prince Shōtoku was in fact a Jōgū, but whole-heartedly with the Soga. He may have felt it unwise, however, to continue living in dense Soga country; at any rate, he constructed a palace at Ikaruga some distance north of the Asuka region and began to build elsewhere in the Home Provinces. Naniwa, never regarded as friendly Buddhist territory, was penetrated, and Shōtoku erected his first temple there, the Shitennō-ji. Other temples that can be historically associated with him—hundreds are said to be—Kōryū-ji in Kyoto, Hōryū-ji in the Ikaruga area, Tachibana-dera in the Asuka region—are widely separated for that time period. His tomb even suggests an attempt to find a permanent resting place conveniently spaced between the temples he had founded.

Fig. 26

The Asuka region lies far south in the Yamato Plain. It is an approximate rectangle, measuring about 12 sq. km. or 3 from north to south and 4 from east to west. Three hills outline it in the north: Amenokaguyama, Miminashiyama and Unebiyama. The plain starts to rise to the south of Asuka toward the Yoshino mountains, and the Asuka River runs diagonally through the region. Its rocky bed provided an abundance of stones for flooring and bases for pillars of buildings and stones for gardens, and its water was easily diverted to the irrigation of rice paddies. Defensively, the area may have been well selected, but practically, it proved to be too remote from the main arteries of both land and sea traffic that criss-crossed farther north.

Kimmei had lived on the very northern edge of the greater Asuka region, if one may use the geographic term in its widest sense, and his successors, until the accession of Empress Suiko, resided in the neigh-bourhood of Sakurai city, in the north-east corner of what later became the Fujiwara capital.

An unbroken line of succession was always the customary claim for Japanese history. This was, in fact, not hard to achieve since each emperor had several wives and numerous offspring, allowing a relatively rich choice. Often a brother was selected, and the eighth century is notable for the number of powerful women who reached the highest office, leading one to suppose that this was the last real fling for the female shamans. The manner of succession was initially complex and rarely bloodless in its early centuries. In intricate manoeuvring, one of the contenders was chosen, serious rivals were often eliminated on pretexts of being against the state, and others, willingly or not, toed the line. The most friendly territory was sought for the location of the palace.

Much of the early history of Japan is best understood in terms of land control. This was an agriculturally-oriented locus complex, common to tribal peoples. The emperor was identified with the palace in which he lived. Although he was usually referred to simply as the emperor, in references to earlier rulers or in formal documents the reference was by location, *i.e.* the emperor who lived in the Okamoto Palace. Their own personal names were only occasionally used. A later sage, one of the ninth century, was charged with the task of assigning posthumous titles to the rulers. These are the names in common use today. The official numbering of the rulers was done in much more modern times, when certain early ones were 'reinstated'.

Buddhism became a central issue in clan rivalry in the early decades after its introduction. Yet it proved to be only a minor threat to the existing practices of Shinto—the Way of the Gods. Educated priests from Korea brought in Chinese religious texts and developed the study of Chinese philosophy and literature. This was accompanied by efforts at the court to apply Chinese legal systems and medical practices.

Buddhism stepped into a vacuum that had been partially created by Shinto's abhorrence of disease, physical mutilation, the sight of blood, and death. Shinto was totally oriented toward life and anything deviating from it was classified as a repulsive pollution. The very word for wound is *kega*, defilement, a Shinto-inspired concept. This is not to say that there was no medical practice in Japan before the advent of Buddhism. Two of the early *kami* (more or less deities, gods, superior spirits) were the founders of medical practice in Japan, and individuals selected for medical training, according to the largely legendary records, were drawn from the highest ranks of the nobility. Obviously, washing and purification were recognized at an early stage as having prophylactic value, and they still stand as mainstays of Shinto custom today. Hot springs attracted the ailing, massaging was indulged in and herb healing was popular. Early Buddhist monks from Korea brought the knowledge of Chinese medicine with them, but it was soon practised by the clergy after the seventh century without the aid of the Korean intermediaries. The Chinese approach to medicine was, in fact, too philosophical for the Japanese, and the Shinto inclination toward incantations and exorcism was soon discovered by the Buddhist clergy to be the quickest way to reach the Japanese interests. Actual practice deteriorated in favour of the magical powers wielded by the priests, and Buddhism came to be widely employed as a protective screen against disease and a cure for sickness. Doctors trained in the government's institutions took over the real medical work as this shift of emphasis occurred. Buddhist temples handled the business of cremations and the memorial services.

In evaluating the accomplishments of the Japanese leadership, it is fairly clear that most of the early emperors were enlightened enough to know what they wanted for the country and to have actually done what they set out to do, namely, to provide it with the best legal, political and cultural systems then known in Asia. In general, these were the systems in practice in China, and throughout the latter half of the seventh century and into the eighth one can see the Japanese inching up the international ladder to an ultimate position that gave the appearance of nominal parity.

As long as the emperor had the energy and freedom of movement to build new palaces, he did not find himself bogged down by the Japanese disposition toward ritual and ceremony. But after the move to Heian (Kyoto) in 794, the system became too bureaucratic and burdensome and finally overwhelmed him. Even before the capital was moved from Heijō (Nara), emperors might retire and then proceed to manage much of the power behind the scenes. Abdication became almost the rule after Empress Jitō (41) left office in 697, seven years before she died.

To survey briefly the events of these centuries is to scan the activities of the great imperial names. Empress Suiko's life involved complicated relationships. She was the third daughter of Emperor Kimmei and the wife of Emperor Bidatsu (30), who was also her half-brother. Bidatsu was succeeded by two of his brothers, Yōmei (31) and Sushun, and she took over following Sushun's assassination. Prince Shōtoku was Yōmei's second son. With official support from the throne, he set about remaking the legal system, establishing rank designations by colour of headgear, building temples, and introducing Chinese customs of other kinds. He was a serious student of Buddhism and a translator of sūtras, which he did, time permitting, at the Ikaruga Palace he had constructed in 601. A temple was later built nearby, the forerunner of one of Japan's greatest ecclesiastical establishments, the Hōryū-ji.

Emperor Kōtoku (36) conspired in the assassination of Soga no Emishi and Soga no Iruka in 645 before taking the throne. The Soga abuse of power left few lamenting their deaths, but contenders for the throne among Prince Shōtoku's family were also eliminated. Kōtoku maintained a palace in Naniwa, an anti-Soga stronghold, and sponsored the Taika Reform (645–646), a sweeping series of changes that regained considerable power for the emperor, was instrumental in appointing officials into a bureaucratic system, set up land allotment methods (*jōri*), regulated taxes, established the census and drastically restricted the building of mounded tombs. He instituted the use of era names (Taika was the first, Great Change). Kōtoku rearranged the ranks in 649, from Shōtoku's twelve to nineteen, and introduced a new system of titles. The top titles were given to the heads of the Abe, Soga and Nakatomi clans, thus recognizing them as the second, third and fourth ranking nobles in the country after the Prime Minister. Their titles were Sadaijin, Udaijin and Naidaijin, Great Minister of the Left, Great Minister of the Right and Great Minister of the Centre.

Some of the persistent rituals of Japan had their beginnings in this period. During Empress Saimei's (37) reign the practice was started of requiring officials to appear at the capitals' temples on the fifteenth day of the seventh month to hear the Urabon-kyō read, the sūtra extolling the virtues of ancestors for seven generations. Out of this developed the well known modern summer Obon Festival, the Feast of the Lanterns.

Emperor Temmu (40) relied fairly heavily on ideas from China, yet also seems to have been able to deal with the kingdom of Silla in Korea, despite its traditional hostility to Japan and its destruction of Paekche in 660. Temmu lived in the Asuka region at Kiyomigahara, and the literature makes mention of so many parts of his palace that scholars have been led to believe that he was the first emperor to have had a fully developed and formal complex of buildings. He standardized the ceremonies of the court, making the best use of the more elaborate architecture—or arranging the architecture to accommodate the elaborate ceremonies. He gave ardent support to the building of temples and quite possibly introduced the new plan in which two pagodas were placed symmetrically in the nucleus of a temple compound. He changed the number of ranks in 682 from the twenty-six that Tenchi (38) had set up in 662 to forty-eight.

Temmu had hoped to move the capital, but death cut short his intentions. It was his wife, who ruled as Empress Jitō, who pushed through the elegant grid plan for the Fujiwara capital and transferred the court in 694. She also had a hand in the writing of the Taihō Civil Code, distributed to the provinces in 701.

The Taihō Civil Code (Taihō-ryō), named after the era name, spelt out the work of the various agencies of the state and the obligations of the officials. The Taihō Penal Code (Taihō-ritsu) followed the Ōmi-ritsu, the penal code issued by Emperor Tenchi while residing in Ōmi, and superseded it in 702 when promulgated. This became the established Nara legal system, and a stable base for a society now absorbing a large dose of Confucian ethic. On the whole, the system was in force until modern times. It was Emperor Mommu (42) who sent instructors to the provinces to describe the provisions of the Civil Code, and he apparently proposed the move of the capital to Heijō. His mother, Empress Gemmyō (43), succeeded him. She carried out the relocation of the capital in 710.

Empress Gemmyō was responsible for the first coins manufactured in Japan, according to the literature, the Wadō-kaichin, in 708, and she also saw to the compilation of the *Kojiki* (Records of Ancient Matters), that came out in 712.

Revisions of the laws were made during the reign of Empress Genshō (44) in the Yōrō era (718), hence the Yōrō-ryōritsu, but application of these seems to have been delayed until after the middle of the century. The *Nihon Shoki* (Chronicles of Japan) was compiled in two volumes in 720, perhaps to make up for the deficiencies recognized in the Kojiki.

Emperor Shōmu (45) is generally regarded as the most culturally-minded of the eighth century emperors. He conceived of building a Great Buddha and constructing an immense temple in the capital, as well as requiring all the provinces to erect temples. The Great Buddha was cast, and the Tōdai-ji, Japan's largest temple, put up. In the process, he cultivated many prominent Buddhist personalities. Civil examinations were made stricter, with appointment resulting from high achievement in the tests. Shōmu is the first known connoisseur of the arts in Japan, and his remarkable collection forms the bulk of the material kept in the Shōsōin, in the grounds of the Tōdai-ji.

The so-called Six Sects of Nara flourished in the latter half of the century. Japanese interests slowly turned inward. Success had been consistently lacking in the military ventures with Korea. Internally, 'barbarians' occupied valuable territory in the Tōhōku region, and several decades were spent trying to drive them farther north. Emperor Kammu (50) was the most successful against these aboriginal people. He was also on the winning side in another war, this one with the Nara priesthood. His victory is marked by the transfer of the capital from Heijō. What the Taika Reform text said about the building of tombs: '. . . the poverty of our people is absolutely owing to the construction of tombs . . .' Kammu was prepared to say about the temples. Various efforts were made to cut their power, including the withdrawal of imperial support, the reduction of their household fiefs and the prohibition of farmers from giving or selling them land. Kammu treated them like the plague; he applied his own brand of Shinto purification and moved away.

The latter half of the century was also a period of economic recession. The war in the north was expensive, the number of appointed officials was becoming burdensome and the monasteries were bulging with able-bodied men. Japan's prosperity was closely tied with that of the T'ang dynasty in China, and the T'ang were experiencing a decline in fortune by the beginning of the ninth century. The Japanese were reaping the fruits of over-exertion, suffering the consequences of the projects of ambitious emperors and the dubious management of female rulers. Most notable in this respect was Empress Shōtoku (48), the same woman as Empress Kōken (46), the daughter of Shōmu. The emperors were strangely susceptible to manipulation by women. The fact that so many empresses emerged at this time is one of the minor embarrassments of Japanese history—a situation that brought on later legislation making it impossible for a woman to occupy the throne. (There were actually two later ones, Myōshō in the seventeenth century and Go-Sakuramachi in the eighteenth.)

After Kammu's decisive action, the palace and court were settled in Heian (Kyoto). The bureaucracy eventually produced a stereotyped form of life within limited national horizons and the emperor's breadth of interest in the country as a whole was replaced by the simple goal of recapturing power. Leading clans fought each other; the emperor intrigued with the most responsive. Natural disasters and wars swept through the capital and wiped out all evidence of its first four hundred years of existence. The oldest buildings standing in Kyoto city today date to no earlier than the Kamakura period (1185–1333).

CHRONOLOGY

Historical divisions are well established by such dated events as reigns, edicts, capital transfers, battles and official foreign contacts. Archaeology adds no precision to these dates, but may shed light on when edicts and laws began to take effect and the characteristics of court and daily life and their material culture. The less precise changes in early art history rarely coincide with historical events; they merely reflect their impact. By and large, the stylistic divisions for these early centuries have been less than satisfactory for two reasons: first, despite the fact that the chief artistic changes were introduced to Japan and not internally contrived, there has always been an effort to correlate them with historic landmarks (after the arrival of Buddhism) which were essentially internal in nature and not necessarily responsible for the stylistic changes; and second, even if an indirect relationship existed, insufficient allowance was made for the time lag between an event and the emergence of a style.

The old names, Suiko, Hakuhō and Tempyō, have been given up in favour of Asuka, Hakuhō and Nara, with a recent effort to replace Hakuhō with Early Nara. Empress Suiko's reign lasted from 592 to 628; Hakuhō is an era name, usually given for the years 673 to 686; Tempyō is also an era name, for the years 729 to 749. Short and non-sequential era names were always inadequate; even Tempyō, which was followed by four successive eras that use Tempyō as a prefix (Tempyō-kampō 749, Tempyō-shōhō 749–757, Tempyō-hōji 757–765, and Tempyō-jingo 765–767), spans only four decades of the eighth century. Hakuhō was awkward at best; it was initially a mistake to apply a single term to what comprises at least two art styles, and Early Nara is a sad choice, since Nara as a city did not exist until 710.

As a consequence of the present state of knowledge, I would favour stylistic subdivisions as shown below, listed against the key monuments that signal the changes. The apprehensive reader will find most of the arguments for this arrangement scattered throughout the text.

Period	Dates	Key Monuments
Early Asuka Period *Introduction of Buddhism : 552*	552–*c.* 585	Insignificant Buddhist production
Middle Asuka Period I *Taika Reform : 645*	*c.* 585–*c.* 660	Asuka⁄dera: 588 Shitennō⁄ji: 593
Middle Asuka Period II	*c.* 660–*c.* 685	Kawahara⁄dera: 660's
Late Asuka Period *Fujiwara Capital : 694 Taihō Civil Code : 701*	*c.* 685–710	Yamada⁄dera Buddha: 685 Yakushi⁄ji: 690's
Early Nara Period *Heijō Capital : 710*	710–*c.* 730	Hōryū⁄ji wall paintings: 710 (?) Hōryū⁄ji pagoda statuettes: 711
Middle Nara Period	*c.* 730–*c.* 760	Kōfuku⁄ji: 730's Tōdai⁄ji: after 745
Late Nara Period *Nagaoka Capital : 784 Heian Capital : 794*	*c.* 760–794	Tōshōdai⁄ji: 760's Saidai⁄ji: after 765; chiefly 770's

CHAPTER II

Coinage and the Economy

Japan's earliest known medium of exchange was rice, in the form of both plants and grain. To this was later added woven cloth, cotton and various other goods until, as a result of observation of methods in China, a system based on gold, silver and copper coins was introduced. But the relative ease with which rice and textiles could be weighed and measured undoubtedly perpetuated their use for business transactions in more outlying areas, despite the government's persistent efforts to promote a wider circulation of metal currency.

The emperors advanced their monetary policies in conjunction with the expansion of official activities throughout the provinces, encouraging travellers to carry money, pay taxes in coins and even, in an edict of 711, offering ranks to enterprising people who would use and acquire coins. As can be imagined, the injunction turned out to have been effectively exploited. It was taken more seriously than anticipated, even private citizens finding collecting to their liking. The provinces then received an order in 798 forbidding the hoarding of coins by individuals and rescinding the offer of ranks to those with socks full of loot. In effect, the initial order had opened up a whole new way of achieving status; it made it possible for an ambitious merchant to elevate himself to positions normally accessible only through family connections before the eighth century. It also compounded the problem of counterfeiting, forcing the government to adopt stringent measures.

The oldest coins found in Japan are Chinese Han dynasty cash of the first century AD. They probably filtered in with Korean immigrants who had some connections with the Chinese colony of Lo-lang in north Korea. The few known examples appear to be grave-goods of the Yayoi period, and could hardly have been more than trinkets, heirlooms or collectors' items to their owners in Japan.

Thousands of Chinese T'ang dynasty coins called K'ai-t'ung yüan-pao, first issued in 621, made their way to Japan. The Japanese prized this coin so highly that they later modelled their own after it. In

Plate 13

fact, the earliest locally made copper coins are almost exactly the same size and design, only inferior in casting. All bear four characters on one side only, to be read clockwise, commencing at the top.

Eleven plain round discs of silver were recovered along with other objects in a small rectangular bronze box when the site of the pagoda of the Sūfuku-ji in Ōtsu city was dug in 1940. These 'coins' (called Mumonginsen, that is, undecorated silver money) most likely had a Korean origin and were a gift to the temple at the time of its dedication in 668. Their weight was standardized by scraping down the surface or, more rarely, adding silver. Nine weigh a little over 2 *momme* (1 momme equals 0.132275 oz. or 3.75 gr.) or close to 9 gr.

Historians have often accepted the date of 708 as the earliest production of copper coins in Japan. In a surge of enthusiasm following the donation of considerable bronze from Chichibu county, Musashi province (Saitama prefecture), the era was renamed Wadō (Refined Copper) to signify the importance of the occasion. The copper coins issued at this time, Wadō-kaichin or Wadō-kaihō,[1] became the standard type and were, in fact, still popular throughout the eighth century, the object of an unusual degree of confidence long lost by later issues.

Silver coins were also included in the Wadō-kaichin series. The records already point out that silver had been donated to the court in 674; minting may have taken place somewhere in the Home Provinces. But the counterfeiting of silver was both too easy and too profitable. It was only a little more than a year following the recorded manufacture of the first silver coins that an imperial edict prohibiting their private production was issued and in the next year their use itself was forbidden altogether, at which time they were recalled from the market.

Fifty years later (760), in another T'ang-inspired effort to facilitate business and stimulate the economy, a further attempt was made to employ silver. Designed for simpler as well as larger transactions, a new issue of copper known as Mannen-tsūhō came out almost simul-taneously; its value was ten times one of the older Wadō-kaichin. In a decimal system, ten of the new copper Mannen-tsūhō coins were equal to one new silver Taihei-genhō, and ten silver Taihei-genhō were in turn equal to one new gold Kaiki-shōhō. In order to receive the copper Mannen-tsūhō, a holder had to turn in ten copper Wadō-kaichin coins at what was obviously an extremely disadvantageous rate.

Preceding the eventful year of Wadō 1 (708), the Nihon Shoki carries a record in the reign of Emperor Temmu corresponding to 683 which orders the use of copper coins while prohibiting the use of silver coins, but this decree was modified only three days later when the ban on silver coins was lifted. Officials of the mint were appointed by Empress Jitō in 694. Certainly the country was moving in the direction of constantly greater dependence on metal currency, and a crucial factor was the directions published in 702 for the standardization of weights and measures throughout the provinces. Several inferences, in other words, though largely textual, have led to the view that coins were already in production before 708.² One might cite the receipt at the court of silver from the province of Iyo (Ehime) in 691 and tin in 698; copper from Inaba (Tottori) and Suō (Yamaguchi) in 698; tin from Iyo and Ise (Mie) in 698. Tsushima (a pair of islands lying between Japan and Korea, always within Japanese sovereignty) was ordered to refine gold ore in 699 and Mutsu (north Honshu) in 701.

This conviction that metal money was being manufactured before 708 is coupled with the assumption that it was based on a Chinese type and each coin was circular with a square hole and was marked with four characters. Most were probably melted down to go into later issues of Wadō-kaichin. But if this is true, why has the year Wadō 1 been so solemnly pronounced from the time of the writing of the Nihon Shoki as the beginning of copper coin production in Japan? In the author's opinion, one possibility is that this date heralds the court's first serious, country-wide attempt to convert from a barter and exchange system to coinage, an effort now founded on the realization that enough copper was known to be available to make the change a practical reality. The ultimate goals, in other words, were worth the pretentious inauguration.

Fig. 2

Copper coins were first minted in Ōmi province (Shiga), but later widely produced, from north Honshu to Kyushu. How legitimate all this production was has yet to be fully determined. Clay moulds and a few unfinished coins have been found, and in at least three sites, two in Yamaguchi prefecture and one in Kyoto prefecture, clay crucibles and bellows as well. The process of manufacture was not difficult; this, combined with their prestige, made Wadō-kaichin always subject to forgery. The sizes vary little, the weights vary more, but the minor differences in the characters are just enough to have prompted suggestions

 Wadō-kaichin (kaihō)
Wadō I (708)

 Mannen-tsūhō
Tempyō-hōji 4 (760)

 Jingō-Kaihō
Tempyō-jingō I (765)

 Ryūhei-eihō
Enryaku 15 (796)

 Fuju-shimpō
Kōnin 9 (818)

 Jōwa-shōhō
Jōwa 2 (835)

 Chōnen-taihō
Kashō I (848)

 Jōeki-shimpō
Jōgan I (859)

 Jōgan-eihō
Jōgan 12 (870)

 Kampyō-taihō
Kampyō 2 (890)

 Engi-tsūhō
Engi 7 (907)

 Kengen-taihō
Tentoku 2 (958)

Fig. 2   The twelve early imperial coins. Average diameter of Wadō-kaichin about 2.5 cm., others to scale. The last three were often so poorly cast that the characters are illegible

that many examples may be the products of local, unauthorized finan-
ciers. Some of the final touches on copper coins were done with a chisel,
as the square holes occasionally show. Examples of the Jingō-kaihō
(issued in 765) bear fine lines running around the outer edges, as though
many coins had been strung together and finished on a simple lathe. In
fact, it is often thought that a square centre hole has few other merits than
the holding of the coins firmly in place with a square-sectioned rod for
just such a finishing operation. The Kaiki-shōhō gold coins were
finished with a metal file individually.

The minting of new copper coins at relatively short intervals during
the latter half of the eighth century and, in fact, more frequently in the
ninth, is reason enough to believe that the economic situation was far
from stable. In all, within the two and a half centuries between the time
the Wadō-kaichin and the last coins were made, twelve copper types
were issued. The most characteristic practice was to withdraw earlier
coins from the market when a new issue was being contemplated and
put out a smaller, and essentially cheaper, series of coins. As this process
undermined confidence in the currency and provoked a steady devalu-
ation, the government ultimately had to face up to a complete reversal of
its monetary policy. Simply enough, the Japanese returned to full
dependence on Chinese coins—at least one aspect of Chinese material
culture for which the Japanese had never lost their high regard. With
increasing dismay the Chinese of the Sung dynasty and others after them
witnessed their coins being hauled off in great quantities by Japanese
traders in exchange for high-priced goods brought over by ship, until
finally the Chinese were forced by 1432 to slow down the process to
protect their own economy.

There are three chief types of Wadō-kaichin coins, a situation
apparently resulting from different places of manufacture and different
time periods. For instance, some Wadō coins contain no lead and only a
little antimony and arsenic. These are most likely the earliest ones.[3]
Examples with a good deal of lead in the composition are thought to be
later. Beginning with the Mannen-tsūhō issue, the percentage of antimony and arsenic increased fairly rapidly. Since this combination of
minerals is not found in Chinese coins, it may be concluded that it is
peculiarly Japanese and the materials were acquired locally.

One can believe that savings were made by the government by reducing the quantity of copper in successive issues. For instance, the 708 Wadō-kaichin contained 90% copper, whereas the 760 Mannen-tsūhō contained only 78%. In records of 819 in regard to the Fuju-shimpō (first issued in 816), it is said that raw materials sent to the mint consisted of 16,333 *kin* (1 kin equals 160 momme or about 1.32 lbs.) of copper and 8.166 kin of lead. If these were alloyed in this proportion, the copper would amount to only about 66%.[4]

No one doubts that many coins were eventually in use. The famous Wadō-kaichin is the most widely dispersed; the great majority and most of the so-called counterfeit coins of the eighth century are of this type. The fact that they are so often found with later coins, in particular with the Mannen-tsūhō and Jingō-kaihō, and other objects, especially pottery, is evidence enough that such coins were zealously treasured. They were frequently used as dedicatory offerings in temples, where they are sometimes found with gold and silver coins and gold plates. As far as can be told, the earliest precisely datable object accompanying recovered Wadō-kaichin coins is a Chinese Huo-ch'üan (Japanese: Kasen) cash of the Han dynasty (Japanese: Yayoi period) from a site in Nagano prefecture, which must, therefore, have been saved for at least seven hundred years, unless it is a later reproduction, which would be very unlikely. The latest datable objects are Engi-tsūhō (907) coins from an Osaka city site.[5]

Sites in the Home Provinces have yielded most of the Wadō-kaichin coins unearthed by archaeologists, especially in the prefectures of Nara, Kyoto, Osaka and Shiga. Unfortunately, many of these finds were made during the pre-scientific period of archaeology and the circumstances of the discoveries are not clear. Regardless of that, there is a preponderance of temples and an occasional shrine in a list of these sites in the Home Provinces and, conversely, very few temples and no shrines in the outer provinces.[6] At the Taima-dera, one Wadō-kaichin, along with Mannen-tsūhō and Jingō-kaihō was encased in a part of the spire of the west pagoda. But in outlying regions, where the practice of burying the dead in tumuli disappeared more slowly, such coins have been found in tombs in the prefectures of Nagano, Gumma, Yamagata and Iwate. Otherwise, they are sometimes associated with cremated remains as side-burials or are found in places of manufacture. An excellent example of the former is the grave of Owarida no Yasumaro at Koōka, Yamabe county, Nara prefecture, composed of a heavy wooden box 44 cm. in length, from which ten silver coins, an inscribed bronze tablet 29.6 cm. in length, datable to 729, an iron object and some Three-coloured pottery (see p. 38) was retrieved.

It is not difficult to explain some of the largest caches as grave-goods buried alongside one or more cinerary urns: 508 Wadō-kaichin coins found in an iron box at Hajishinden, Sakai city, Osaka prefecture; 201 with pottery vessels at Furuichi, Katahara-chō, Nara city, and 300 with reddish pottery at Ōharano village, Otokuni county, Kyoto prefecture, for instance. But the single Wadō-kaichin coin which came to light in a pit-dwelling at the Funabashi site, Osaka, may well be nothing more than a misplaced piece of money, lost forever by some middle-class owner when the house was abandoned. One of the most interesting discoveries is the collection of 71 Wadō-kaichin, some of which are silver, 83 Mannen-tsūhō and 280 Jingō-kaihō coins found together at Okijima, Ōmihachiman city, Shiga prefecture, a lake-bottom site which Satō thinks was probably a mint.[7] Incidentally, a silver Taihei-gempō was found in one of the wooden store-houses of the Tōshōdai-ji in 1928.

The decrees on using coins and establishing prices carry with them obvious implications regarding the wide circulation of coins, even granted the known centralization of the Nara period government. A 709 order specified that goods worth four *mon* or more be purchased in silver coins, and goods worth less in copper coins. The rice price was then fixed at one mon in coin for six *shō* (1 shō equals 1.8039 litres). By 764 the price of rice had been set at one thousand copper coins for one *koku* (100 shō) and when new coins went on the market the next year the old coins were kept in circulation. The impression one receives is that an imperial order inferring the use of one thousand coins in a single transaction is in effect saying that a considerable amount of ready cash was thought to be available.

New issues may have been designed to reduce counterfeiting, and counterfeiters were severely dealt with. But many of the common practices of the day were unlikely to contribute toward a balanced budget. It is generally conceded that the officials in outlying districts lived more comfortably than those in the Home Provinces, where conditions were crowded and the complaint was constantly heard that the tribute did not get through. Many edicts were phrased, more land assigned, an increase in crops encouraged, prices and interest rates raised, methods to keep people in debt to the government devised, conscientious farmers rewarded, and weaving instructors dispatched to the provinces to provide more and a greater variety of textiles. The census was frequently taken, additional supervisors were appointed, and one could name more ways that were intended to see that the taxes reached the capital. But these measures were more often than not cancelled out by unreliable officials or the pecuniary ways of those living off the government. The officials had a tendency to line their own pockets or to attach to them-selves unauthorized land (*viz.* edicts of 705, 712, 761, 765, 784 and 785); people registered themselves as members of a household residing in the capital in order to be exempt from many taxes; temples had avid appetites for land not allotted to them through regular channels (*viz.* edicts of 713, 746, 784 and 785); monks were periodically upbraided for their evil, often unspecified, ways, not the least of which were acquisitive habits (*viz.* edicts of 717, 722, 780 and 798, the last of which was an investigation of their unsavoury practices). Many monks were more or less impressed into service—frequently done to alleviate the illness of a sovereign or to avert a national disaster, as in 725 when 3,000 people were obliged to enter monasteries and nunneries—so it need not be thought that all were in the cloister because of a passionate desire to serve the Buddha as intercessors for their fellow men. In fact, many lawless individuals masqueraded as monks, resulting in identification cards being issued to authenticated monks in 720 and 724. Temples and their inhabitants were among the chief hoarders, as both the old records and modern archaeology have graphically shown.

Gold or gilt bronze objects had been known in Japan since the Yayoi period, but local Japanese production cannot be proved until a rather late date. Numerous horse trappings, jewellery and other objects recovered from tumuli attest to the popularity of gold work among the aristocrats of the Tomb period, and many early gilt bronze Buddhist statues ranging from portable to life-size still enhance the interior of temples and museums today. There can be little doubt that the court and nobles made every effort to ensure the availability of gold in Japan.

The 694 order to officials of Tsushima to refine gold speaks for the existence of an active trade in the ore through Korea and the likelihood that employable goldsmiths lived there. For the main islands, however, such an order comes no earlier than 701. In that year an official was sent to Mutsu to refine gold. No more is heard of this particular man; success is not reported until 749, at which time, with all due fanfare, represen-tatives presented gold to the court. This event is often taken as the first time gold was locally worked in Japan.[8] Parenthetically, gold was sent to the court from Shizuoka in the following year, but the people of north Honshu had made the mistake of boasting of their new-found wealth; they were now allowed to pay their regular tribute in commodities, but commuted taxes had to be paid in gold. Not only that, but certain people were required to contribute the equivalent of ten grams. From a realistic viewpoint most laws were difficult to enforce despite census after census, and practically speaking, much of this region was occupied by the Ainu and therefore hostile territory. But at the worst, the decree was designed to guarantee a steady if not large supply from the north.

It would be hard to imagine gold coins passing through many hands. The chances are slight that anyone other than imperial relatives, higher officials and temple managers actually saw them, much less handled them. The Kaiki-shōhō had a diameter of 2.64 cm., that is, slightly greater than the 10 yen coin in use today, the largest current denomination. The recovery of one of these gold coins from the site of the west pagoda of the Saidai-ji in 1794 caused enough flutter to have been entered in the records. This huge eighth century temple, located in the northwest corner of Nara city, built by Empress Shōtoku, met its demise at an early date when its imperial support failed as the power centre shifted hands. Digging that took place in the vicinity of the temple in 1936 was responsible for bringing to light 31 more gold coins—perhaps a little scrap of evidence that the temples were not wholly innocent of the charges of hoarding.

Shinto Ritual Sites and Ceramic Wares

There are hundreds of sites scattered around the country where Shinto rituals have been and in some cases still are being practised. Relics found at these sites that can be identified as ritual types go back no farther than the Tomb period. It is probably no over-simplification to say that all early, traditional, non-Buddhist religious practices can be called Shinto. These resulted from beliefs that were rooted exclusively in localized animistic concepts and so were peculiar to Japan alone. Shinto, popularly called The Way of the Gods, takes a general view of deities or higher spirits (*kami*) as being in and around unusual features of nature. Its practices were surprisingly uniform at an early date—if the similarity of certain types of objects in ritual sites is sufficient indication—because of their spontaneity and simplicity, characteristics shared by other early agricultural societies elsewhere in the world.

Even after Buddhism was secure no Shinto practices were abandoned. Offerings were made at the shrines and elsewhere to the local *kami* on annual and emergency occasions, while prayers were still read at the temples. But Buddhism's future became more assured when it reduced its competition with Shinto by outgrowing its magical attitude. Shinto dealt with ways of exorcism, protection of life, crops and property, and fertility; in other words, with security and the good life in general. In the early centuries of Shinto, the means of arriving at the desired results were more or less the same from place to place. It was the increase in population and complexity of life that gave rise to the proliferation of folk beliefs in later centuries, dealing with *kami* of mountains, rice fields, the sea, the household, and the roads used by travellers. These increases account for the greater diversity in the practices, but inasmuch as their

Fig. 3   Haji pot with human face painted in black ink, probably for ritual use, from Matsubara city, Osaka prefecture. Height 14.2 cm. Second half of eighth century

underlying beliefs had no founder, no early organization and were arrived at collectively and followed instinctively by the common people, and all recognized the presence of *kami*, they too may be included in the wider definition of Shinto.

Fig. 4

Most Shinto ritual sites show this direct relationship to the natural topography. They are associated with mountains, passes, rivers, streams, springs, lakes, ponds, islands, cliffs, rocks and trees. Since spirit life was believed to exist in the vicinity of these phenomena, offerings were made at or near spots thought to be the most sacred.

Fig. 3

Relics at such sites are often loosely scattered because of the way the votive gifts were offered, and today there may be no surface indications of their presence. Rarely were the gifts actually buried. By and large they were gently thrown into the holy spot. Some were pitched into water, such as into wells or pools and rivers, while others were hung on trees. Offerings were also placed on a little table, tray or shelf. More than one of these ways was often used, and all are still seen today. It need hardly

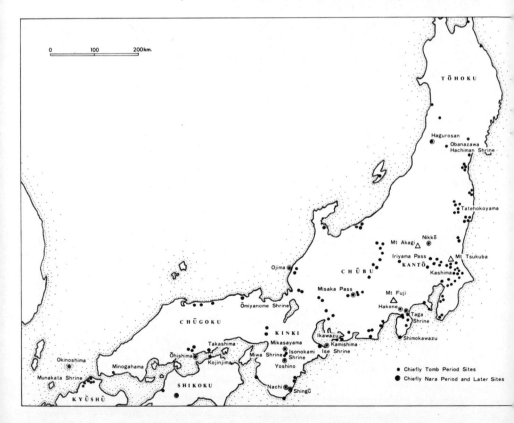

be said that practices of this sort may disperse the relics widely, yet
stratigraphy has been found in some sites and chronological changes in
types and quality of gifts have been noted.

While many different kinds of objects have been recovered from these
ritual sites, the one class common to most are the replicas in clay and
stone. These are chiefly of mirrors and swords or knives, and sometimes
of animals. They belong to a replica tradition that goes back to the early
tumuli of the fourth century AD.

Plate 7

A cursory look might be taken at three of the great ritual sites in widely
separated parts of the country where their varying periods of use depended
on the traffic conditions in each area. One is the Okitsu-gū (Inner
Shrine) of the Munakata Shrine, on Okinoshima, an island lying
between Japan and Korea; the second is the three Kumano shrines in the
south-eastern part of the Kii peninsula, one of which grew up near the
famous Nachi Waterfalls; and the third is Misaka Pass, a treacherous
spot along an old road that ran between Nagano and Gifu prefectures.

Okinoshima, a sacred island on which is situated one of three associated shrines, was an offering site for seafarers plying between Japan and
Korea and of great importance when Japan was still hoping for trade
with or conquest of its nearest neighbour. The supervision of the rituals
may have been directly under the Yamato government. Bronze mirrors
and horse trappings and other objects of exceptional quality were
deposited under many overhanging rocks and never touched again.
Removal was prohibited and, except for a thin mantle of natural deposit
of soil, they are just as they were laid. The rock ledges are traditionally
looked on as *iwakura* or 'seats of the gods.' The sanctity of the place is even
today maintained, despite the removal of the relics by archaeologists, by
still prohibiting women to set foot on the island.

Pottery is rarely mixed with the metal objects under the rocks. What
is found in open sites is Sue ware, the customary ritual pottery of the
Tomb period, or the type that would have been used by the ordinary
sailor on his way through if he wished to make an offering of food.

Other than the quality of its metal offerings, Okinoshima's own
speciality are the simple steatite replicas of humans, horses and boats. The
boats were undoubtedly used to gain favour with the *kami* for safe
voyages. These replicas lost their realism in the course of time and
tapered off into cheap, abstract productions.

◄ *Fig. 4 Major Shinto ritual sites*

After the Nara period, when the court had lost interest in Korea, most of the officiating at these shrines was probably taken over by the Munakata clan,[1] accounting for the decline in quality of the offerings to the level seen at most popular ritual sites. A small number of objects of a later date were recovered. For instance, sixteen coins of the Sung dynasty were unearthed at Site No. 4.

The Kumano region grew into an attractive Shinto pilgrimage centre in medieval centuries for people from Nara and Kyoto, fostered by a strong Ryōbu-shinto (Dual-aspect Shinto, in which Shinto *kami* are identified with Buddhist deities, or vice-versa) development. Among the many sacred spots, offerings were made near the foot of the falls at Nachi and around the rocks along the sloping path leading to the falls. The region reached its height of popularity in the Kamakura period, when it came to be regarded as a vast mandala, a concept that is portrayed in many paintings.

The first finds in modern times are said to have been accidentally exposed in 1918 when logs that had been slid off the hillside by lumber-jacks overturned large rocks near the foot and perhaps ripped through one or more sūtra mounds. These objects include eight bronze Buddhist statuettes in the Late Asuka and Nara style and six in the Heian style. Part of a halo may be even earlier. Since Nachi has yielded no other evidence of early rituals, these pieces are either copies made during the Kamakura period or heirlooms finally consigned to a mound or some other kind of cache. As archaisms, the Nachi figures would be far from unique. Reproducing earlier types was a good business in the Kama-kura period, and heirlooms are always the jokers in historic assemblages.

Recent excavations under boulders have brought to light the typical Shinto objects of mirrors, swords and beads, along with some brown celadon, Kamakura period pottery from Sanage and elsewhere, and Sung dynasty coins.

Misaka Pass, called the Pass of the Gods, reflects long use and the slow pace of change in the rituals. Several sites are situated along the old Tōsan road, a road that had become an official artery in the fifth century and remained in general use for about 700 years. Misaka was considered to be one of the most precipitous and perilous points along the route, and the spirits inhabiting the area were rather hostile unless placated by the traveller. Even the famous warrior Yamato-takeru no mikoto (Yamato-

Plate 8

Plate 6

dake) had difficulty getting through. The Manyōshū includes a poem
which spells out a traveller's fears:

> *At Misaka, the Pass of the Gods,*
> *I have made offerings,*
> *Praying for the safety of my life—*
> *All for my mother's and father's sake.*   xx: 4402[2]

The site covers a fairly large and rather flat area just north of the highest
point (elevation 1570 m.) of the pass. A popular idea in more recent
times that has looked on anyone who picked up a bead in transit as being
in line for good fortune has, needless to say, been less than fortunate for
the site. The first serious investigation of the area was made in 1952, and
an excavation was carried out in 1966. The most recent excavation,
conducted in 1968, served to establish the chronology and full character
of the relics.

Among the great quantity of potsherds, the oldest distinctively ritual
pieces are Haji and Sue of the fifth century AD, the latter increasing in
number from the late seventh into the ninth century. The pottery came
from kilns in Gifu and Aichi prefectures, especially the extensive Sanage
kilns in Aichi, and was left there by passers-by on their way to the
eastern coastal provinces. This was, in fact, the route by which most of
the Sanage wares reached the Kantō region. Some green-glazed sherds
(only 104) of the last excavation, date from the ninth to the eleventh
centuries and were probably products first of Gifu and later of Aichi
kilns. This green glaze is in the direct tradition of the Three-colour ware
of the Nara period, and it still retained much the same identification with
aristocracy that the Three-colour had in Nara times.

The greatest amount of pottery is the widely used, commercially made,
tenth century ash-glazed ware of the Sanage kilns. There are sixteen
pieces of Chinese porcelain, but these are of uncertain date. When the
Kiso bypass was opened up around the twelfth century, the quantity of
offerings dropped off fairly rapidly, and the pottery that was left was of
types from closer kilns. The travellers were fewer and apparently
consisted of merchants making local trips. Once Misaka Pass could be
circumvented not many people bothered to use it and those who did felt
only nominal obligations to the *kami*. There are no relics dating to after
the fifteenth century.

Plate 7
The stone replicas at Misaka may have been placed there by travellers from the Kantō. The replica practice probably originated in the Kansai, but it burgeoned in the Kantō, where the production and sale of the little stone objects by the roadside must have become a rather respectable business. There are few replicas thought to post-date the eighth century, but this is not to say that they may not have been made and used in perishable, and perhaps more transportable, materials. Many objects are perforated, leading one to believe that a common way of making offerings at Misaka Pass was by hanging the gift on a tree. The pottery after the eighth century is not of ritual varieties. It was probably the personal property of the traveller or was being transported for commercial use. He selected any piece he felt he could spare.

T'ang dynasty Three-colour ware was introduced to Japan by the eighth century and was soon reproduced locally. Several pieces of Three-colour have been found on Okinoshima, the last in 1969, which seem to be Chinese. The basic colours of the lead glaze are green, brown and white, with variations in the brown from a reddish to yellow.
Fig. 5
Japanese preference was for two or even just the green colour alone, and the 57 pieces of this type in the Shōsōin, of local manufacture, are largely two- or one-colour vessels.

Excavations in recent years have recovered many sherds from such eighth century temple sites as the Kōfuku-ji, Daian-ji and Saidai-ji in Nara, an abandoned temple at Furuichi in Nara prefecture, another in Kashiwara city, Osaka prefecture, and Heijō Palace. So far the Japanese-made Three-colour ware itself is found only in the capital area or, like Okinoshima, if it is Japanese, where the government had vested interests. Other parts of the country had the related two- or one-colour wares, made at several kilns. Despite the Shōsōin's paucity of Three-colour pieces—where there should be nothing else—the Three-colour was without doubt an aristocratic ware shared only with a few court-controlled and private temples.

One of the largest, if not the largest, single supplier of pottery from late prehistoric times to the end of the Kamakura period (1185–1333) was the Sanage area in Aichi prefecture where hundreds of kilns produced for a market that eventually encompassed two-thirds of the country. The Sanage kilns were located in the counties of Nishi-kamo and Aichi, north-east of Nagoya city, in a low, hilly area about 20 km.

Fig. 5 Two-colour drinking bottle (green and yellow glaze), from Nanatsu Pond, Oharada-chō, Kōriyama city, Fukushima prefecture. Height 28.9 cm. Eighth or early ninth century

square. They took their name from Sanage-yama, the mountain that lies across the borders of Owari and Mikawa provinces. The entire region was rich in 'porcelain' clay; it served the thousands of kilns around the cities of Komaki, Seto and Tokoname. Sanage's own kilns numbered about 1,170.[3]

When a waterway development got underway to lead to expanded cultivation of the region, the area was dug from 1955–62, primarily by Nagoya University, with remarkable techniques resulting for determining stratigraphy in abandoned kiln sites.

The oldest kilns produced Sue ware in the fifth century in typical Tomb period shapes, made from reddish clay containing iron. While no actual kilns of Sue ware have been excavated at Sanage, standard hillside Sue kilns are known to have been built on a gentle slope. There are no kilns definitely datable to the sixth century, but manufacture of pottery could hardly have let up at that time. One product of unexpected

39

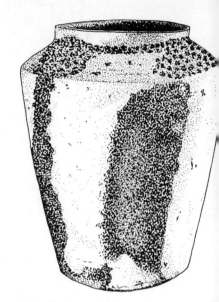

Fig. 6   Pottery vessels from Sanage kilns, Aichi prefecture; (left) diameter 9.2 cm.; late eighth or early ninth century; and (right) height 17.2 cm.; late seventh or early eighth century

popularity, which tells as much about the art of writing as the old literature, were 'ink-stones'. They were made in quantity starting with the late Tomb period, and many have been found at Heijō Palace.

Fig. 21

Sanage wares reached larger markets in the early seventh century, yet only 27, or 9%, of the datable kilns belong to the period ranging from the fifth to the early eighth centuries. In building a kiln a ditch was first dug up a hillside. Walls and roof resembling a barrel vault were then built over it of straw-tempered clay. A late seventh century kiln, no. 17 in the Iwasaki sector of Sanage, ascended a 29° slope and was 13.7 m. in length, 1.6 m. in width and 1.5 m. in height internally.[4]

Fig. 6

Business flourished spectacularly from about the middle of the Nara period into Early Heian, when 162 (out of 300 datable) kilns were in use. The bottle shapes took on features peculiar to Sanage, and a special kind of low, flat-bottomed pouring pot with stubby spout began to be made. More than 16 kilns produced little model pagodas during this stage. With expansion, the better quality silty clays in the east of the area were used. Ash-glazing appeared on the bottle shapes from the late Nara period, which were fired between 1,240° and 1,250°C., and Sanage pottery started to show up well beyond the confines of the eastern coastal region, ranging in sites all the way from the Chūgoku to the Tōhoku. An example of the latter are the Sanage fragments at Taga-jō.

Early Heian kilns (ninth century) averaged 8 m. in length and 1.3 m. wide. They sloped as much as 40°, the steepest angle at Sanage, but returned to about 22° after the tenth century. Little clay supports were placed under the vessels during the firing.

Long-necked bottles and especially types with egg-shaped bodies are ninth to tenth century productions. The latter adhered more closely to the shape of the metal prototype at Sanage than elsewhere; they were in demand for use in temples and offices in the Home Provinces. Green glaze was applied to Sue vessels fired around 750° in the middle Heian period and various kinds of flat plates were manufactured in quantity. From that time until Late Heian, many pots, bowls and plates bear finely incised floral patterns.

Glazing increased in prevalence and the peak of production was reached after the mid-tenth century. Much glazed ware in relatively good quality clay intended for daily use was transported out of Sanage following the Late Heian period. By Kamakura times the so-called Yamachawan were being made. These were simple tea bowls. From the late tenth century until around the early Muromachi period (1392–1573) about 800 kilns were kept in operation. In later stages mass production forced a return to cheaper clays and the area was eventually abandoned in favour of Seto and Tokoname.

Fig. 7

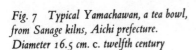

Fig. 7 Typical Yamachawan, a tea bowl, from Sanage kilns, Aichi prefecture. Diameter 16.5 cm. c. twelfth century

41

CHAPTER IV
Land Allotment, City Planning and Administration

The regular disposition of units of land under eminent domain in rural areas is called the *jōri* system and in the cities the *jōbō* system. The basic concept was fixed by theory and afforded only minor variations in practice, for instance, in the numbering of squares and amount of space assigned to each inhabitant.

The method was devised for equitable distribution of newly available land, the preparation of which was of considerable expense to the govern-ment, but from which, therefore, a fixed amount of produce could be expected and, consequently, a fixed amount of taxes annually. There were advantages to the government in keeping the land from falling into the hands of either the private landowners, from whom it was more difficult to extract taxes, or the temples, which were exempt from such taxes or had their own lands already working to support them.

Fig. 8

In open, relatively level areas, the physical result of this apportioning system was a checkerboard of rice fields, composed of 36 squares within a larger square. Read in the north-south direction, the squares were *jō*; in the east-west direction, they were *ri*. In a city they were *jō* and *bō*. As shown in the diagram, the reduction of space was done in a number of ways. Each of the small 36 squares was a *tsubo*, which was 6 by 6 *shaku*. A shaku is close to an English foot; it and the tsubo remained the units of measurement until only a few years ago.

In the Taika Reform, Article 3, the size of rice fields were specified as 30 *bu* in length and 12 bu in width, making one *tan*. It was on the basis of a tan that fields were assigned to workers. The same article set a limit of 50 houses to a township, supervised by a head man, and said that a person should be able to own the fields nearest his house.

Land allotment was designed to provide support for the government with goods in kind and adequate security for the farming class. Each free man above the age of five received 2 tan; each female above the same age received 1⅓ tan. Nominally, at least, the state kept the interests of the people at heart. There were frequent remissions of taxes for hardship conditions or meritorious service, and even generous donations, such as

42

gifts of iron hoes to needy or deserving groups. But the taxes, and especially what amounted to conscription, worked a great burden on many young men who often found it easier to attach themselves to a wealthy landowner and in that way escape some of the state's obligations.

More and more land passed into private hands and the aristocrats and temples benefited the most through favours and exploitable irregularities in the system of immunities. The burdens on the peasants increased. A worker beholden to the state became virtually enslaved by the pressure to produce and the mounting interest rates on what he had borrowed. It could be said that to all intents and purposes the system was not working by the end of the century and it was abandoned after the capital was moved to Heian.

Actual application of the jōri system must have taken some time. The best evidence for its application is the location of the Kawahara-dera, a temple in Asuka known to have been in operation in the 660's. It was oriented north and south and conformed to the blocked-out system. Full and indisputable application is apparent by 694 when Empress Jitō

Fig. 8 Diagrams of jōri system, showing basic units of land allotments, numbering methods and subdivision of squares

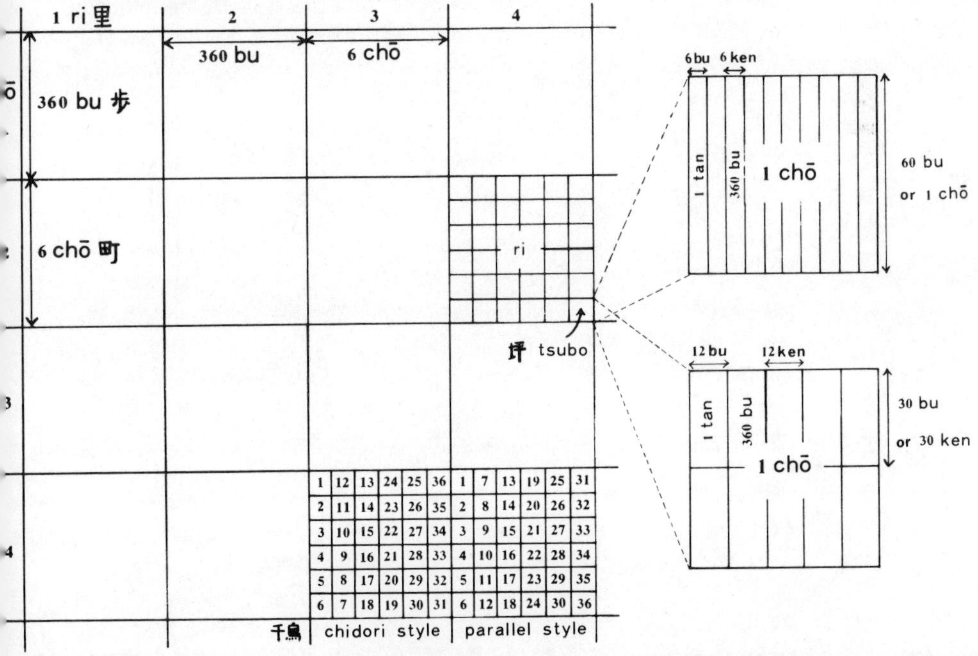

moved into the grid-plan Fujiwara capital. During the eighth century the jōri system was widespread, but it died out in the Heian period when crown lands began to disappear.

The system is known especially in the Yamato region and in other places noted for their concentrations of tumuli. In other words, the old tribal areas were brought under a unified legal system in the middle of the seventh century. Even today, villages laid out in this manner can be seen in the Home Provinces, skirted by regular fields. Jōri remains are known as far north as the modern city of Sendai, in the Inland Sea region, in the Izumo area on the opposite side of Honshu and scattered all the way down to south Kyushu.

The present shape of rice fields and the frequent survival of old names that include the words 'jō', 'ri' or 'tsubo' have been guides for archae-ological work on this system. At Monju village, Ashuha county, Fukui prefecture, land was kept in the name of the Tōdai-ji of Heijō, pinpointed as south-west 8 jō, 6 ri, 12 tsubo. It was found to have had its paddies built with a deep-set layer of intrusive soil, doubtless laid for this purpose.[1]

The Chinese used the block plan of a city to control its inhabitants. The Japanese must have had the same idea in mind, but the physical difference between a Chinese and a Japanese capital city was con-siderable. Without walls, stone and brick buildings, a Japanese city appeared less fortress-like, rather temporary, but more spacious. Little more than pagodas broke the Japanese skyline.

Fujiwara's blocks were rectangular, like those of Ch'ang-an. The north-south dimension of each Fujiwara block was doubled for Heijō, producing squares, and a scheme that has been pointed to with pride as making Heijō more Japanese than Fujiwara.[2]

Fig. 9

The Japanese capitals had a city master (*zōkyō-shi*), a chief master (*rei*) for every four blocks, and a master (*chō*) for each individual block. From chief ministers down to so-called inferior households, space assignments were made on the basis of rank and number of able-bodied men to a household. Space allotments were sometimes cut in half during the eighth century and in some cases reduced by half again before the century was out.[3] Each new city illustrates an acute awareness of the space problems and, consequently, smaller allotments, to a degree resembling ghetto conditions.

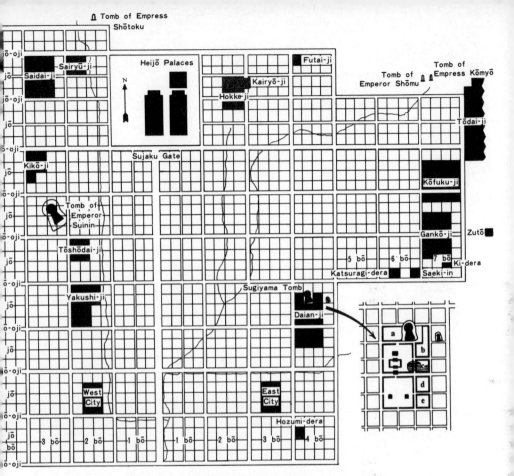

Fig. 9 The capital of Heijō in the eighth century with enlargement of Daian-ji to show how its blocks were used: (a) refectory and administration buildings, (b) servants' quarters, (c) garden, (d) storehouses, (e) fields.

The temples were fitted into the blocks of the city and oriented with its lines. The same held true for country temples which, after this time, were oriented due north and south.

The Ikaruga-dera, the first Hōryū-ji, lay on an axis about 20° west of north. The buildings, probably of a palace, under the Hokki-ji followed the same lines, but the temple itself, built after 685, was constructed on a north-south axis. The main gates of the Daian-ji and at least the two pagodas of the Saidai-ji conformed admirably to the block system in

45

Fig. 50

Heijō city but, outside the city, the cloisters of the Tōdai-ji's pagodas were rather seriously misaligned.

Rather intriguing is the fact that in the Gekyō, the Outer Capital, which at Heijō projected three large blocks to the east in the northern half of the city, the axis of the Kōfuku-ji was well aligned. This large temple was begun along the eastern edge of the city in 710, and must have been started as the city was being laid out. The shaku (foot) unit of measurement for the Outer Capital was a fraction shorter than it was for the city proper and so produced rectangular blocks. The first reaction to this is to imagine that the Outer Capital was added later. While this may possibly be true, it could also be the case that the Kōfuku-ji was laid out precisely north and south as a result of practices employed since the founding of the Fujiwara capital, but the shaku had to be slightly modified in order to fit the temple squarely within these eastern blocks.

Projecting from the north-west corner of Heijō was a section called Hokuhenbō (North border blocks). It was probably added after the construction of the Saidai-ji, which had been ordered by Empress Shōtoku in 765. Its units of measurement were the standard ones for the city as a whole.

Grid-plan provincial cities (*kokufu*) were built in many provinces to enable the government to maintain its local offices. These varied in size, indicating that there was no express order from headquarters on size and details. Notably large among these cities were those of Suō (Yamaguchi prefecture), Ichizen (Ishikawa), Ōmi (Shiga) and Ise (Mie).

Within these provincial cities, the provincial offices (*kokuga*) and sub-provincial offices (*gunga*) may have vaguely resembled palaces in the middle of the checkerboard scheme. The sub-provincial office of Hitachi was dug at Niihari in Ibaragi prefecture between 1941 and 1943. Three of its four groups of buildings comprised various kinds of store-houses.[4] No tiles were found, but stone bases seem to have been in use.[5]

Fig. 10

VILLAGES

Plate 3

Modern suburban housing developments, for which huge areas of farmland have been bought up and bulldozed, have revealed for the first time the layout of villages of the late prehistoric and early historic periods. One of the most extensive of these is the Tama River lowland Funada site within the jurisdictional area of Hachiōji city, in the far western suburbs of Tokyo.

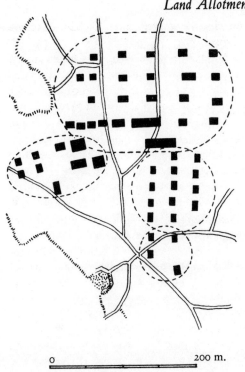

N

Fig. 10   Plan of Provincial Office of Hitachi province, at Nīihari, Kyōwa village, Makabe county, Ibaragi prefecture. Offices and houses lie to the west, storage buildings in the other directions. Eighth century

0   200 m.

During a period of about ten months in 1968 and 1969, excavations were pressed to stay ahead of the construction plans, and about 340 pits of houses were dug. Of greatest importance is the fact that roughly 100 of these belong to historic centuries, a number that far exceeds anything found at any other site of a similar time period.

Occupation of the area started in the Middle Jōmon period, for which two pit-dwellings are the evidence, but occupation was not continuous until perhaps after the late Yayoi period (18 houses), and gives the appearance of lasting without a break into the Heian period (ninth century). There are 20 pits of houses of the early Tomb period, 199 of the late Tomb period, 83 of the early historic, and 18 of even later times.[6]   Plate 2 The most use was made of the area from the late fifth to the eighth centuries.

47

At first glance the historic period pits of dwellings look poorer than the earlier ones, and their relationship suggests that Funada was a middle class community with its controls coming from outside. The social organization is not immediately apparent. The pits of historic houses are scattered throughout the site; there were no special groupings of houses, no large buildings, and no unusual caches of relics. The house pits are shallow and fairly small, averaging about 4 by 4 m. Unlike Tomb period houses, they lack post-holes and storage pits. Almost every house has some pottery and iron tools. Much of the pottery is Sue ware, which was converted more to domestic use as fewer mounded tombs were built. The quantity of Sue ware increased with time and some households owned good quality Sue vessels brought in from distant kilns. The recovery of an occasional coin implies that at least a few of the residents honoured the wishes of the government in carrying out their transactions.

It is almost axiomatic in such locations that a growing population brought on a reduction in the size of the houses, and there must have been some trend towards surface-dwellings. The lack of post-holes probably means that light-weight frame houses were built over a depressed floor, and the absence of storage pits speaks for more and better pottery and perhaps community storehouses, although the remains of storehouses have yet to be identified. Tumuli are not known in the area. Perhaps the village was free of the physical presence of the controlling nobility during the Tomb period and the dead were simply buried in holes in a nearby cemetery. This, or possibly a modest amount of cremation, may have continued in the early historic centuries.

Where the jōri system existed, villages inevitably fitted into the regular scheme. Application of the system would have taken place once the administration to handle it was established in the area. By way of illustration, rows of post-holes are 29° off the jōri lines at the Shima site in Yamagata city, a village known to have flourished in the seventh century.[7] The logical conclusion is that the jōri system had not yet been put into effect at the time the village was occupied. On the other hand, at the Kinotsubo (Hiraki) site, Yamato county, Fukuoka prefecture, where Nara and Heian period pit-dwellings are chiefly round or square with rounded corners and have an average size of about 3 m. in diameter, the pits fit a square of the jōri system. In other words, the houses belonged to a planned village.[8]

Small villages down to hamlet size ranged between five and fifteen houses. The Kusakabe site in Yamanashi had two rows of pits forming sixteen dwellings of the Late Asuka and Nara periods. All but three were very small. At the Irino site, Tano county, Gumma prefecture, two pits were large, one was medium and two were small. The small ones were close to the largest ones, while the largest had the richest remains. The clustering may have been due to related family units.[9]

Assuming that few pit-dwellings would hold more than five people, an estimate might be for an average of twenty people to a cluster of houses, an estimate which is also borne out by texts dealing with taxes,[10] land allotment and disposition of property. In a realistic accommodation to the population increase, formal villages, first limited to thirty houses, were enlarged to fifty houses after the Taika Reform, and the head man, the coordinator of community activities, assigned to the village, found his duties almost doubled by the change.

Each village had at least one communal, nearby well, and presumably a shrine. *Fudoki* writers were entrusted with recording the local scene, but when the Hitachi Fudoki speaks of Ukishima village having nine shrines, it does so with a tone of amazement.

Houses themselves are known to have been built in several styles in the Tomb period, as a quick look at the *haniwa* will show. Any later structural modifications were not very great. An eighth century document describing property for sale confirms the belief that some houses had grass-thatched or board roofs, board walls and wooden floors.[11]

Plate 1

CHAPTER V

Military Headquarters and Fortifications

The government's southern outpost, built as its military centre for defence against what was thought to be a hostile partnership of Korea and China after Japan lost its allies in the peninsula, was Dazaifu, where outlines of roads and fields still show a checkerboard plan today. The earthen ramparts for the citadel were constructed in the reign of Emperor Tenchi (664), which is virtually the only known date regarding the beginning of the complex. In any case, Dazaifu served primarily during the eighth century as the political and military headquarters of the south.

In current fashion, the city was divided into an eastern half (Sakaku) and western half (Ukaku). A jōbō system of at least 22 jō and 12 bō for each half is implied in an old text,[1] while another text speaks of it as a huge, bustling metropolis and gives the impression that it was the largest city west of Heijō (Nara). The administrative section occupied 4 chō in the north.

Dazaifu's nerve centre was the Tofurō (Tower of the City), a cluster of axially-arranged buildings with a seven by four bay Main Hall with base stones carved in two steps, a rear hall, a pair of halls on east and west, and two gates in the front. The bays of the Main Hall were almost one-third longer on the east and west ends than on the north and south sides, but in the case of the latter were slightly narrower at either end. The building, therefore, probably had a structural and bracketing system that resembled the main hall of an eighth century temple in Heijō.

Another group of buildings stood to the east. Dazaifu is the term applied literally to these two groups of buildings, but by extension is used for the city as a whole.[2] Five temples were constructed inside the city—two of which are unidentifiable by name today—and four stood in the immediate vicinity, including the Provincial Temple and its related nunnery.

Fig. 11

Plate 10

SOUTHERN FORTIFICATIONS

Two castles, Ōno-jō (jō equals castle) in the Dazaifu area, and Ki-jō in Motoyama-chō, Saga prefecture, were built as flanking protection for

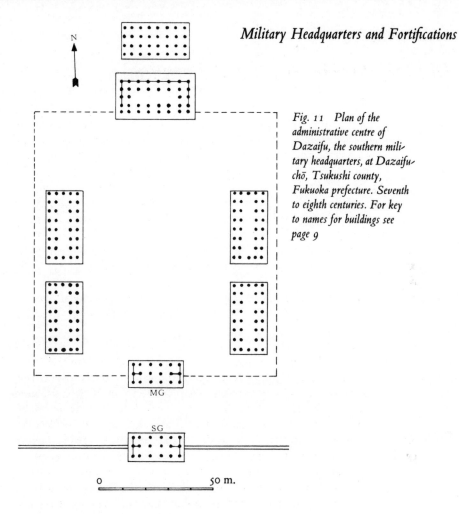

N

Fig. 11   Plan of the administrative centre of Dazaifu, the southern military headquarters, at Dazaifu-chō, Tsukushi county, Fukuoka prefecture. Seventh to eighth centuries. For key to names for buildings see page 9

MG

SG

0   50 m.

Dazaifu, and a third, Ito-jō, was constructed between 764 and 776 under the direction of Koreans from Paekche, presumably to provide for defence of the coast. Other than meagre scraps of information, the ancient documents are singularly uninformative about the fortifications of southwestern Japan. Archaeological work can hardly cover the vast terrain occupied by these defences and, despite a good deal of digging, numerous questions remain to be answered.

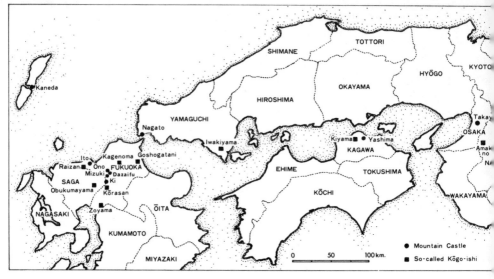

Fig. 12   Early fortifications in south-west Japan

There is a dearth of datable objects from these sites, but since the features of the fortifications are distinct from those of obviously later castles and have Korean connections, they should belong to an early period of Japan's relations with Korea and, moreover, to a time when these relations were less than cordial. An occasional local ruler in Kyushu had dreams of independence and one, Iwai, was believed to have had covert dealings with Silla, the kingdom in the south-east part of the peninsula. His activities culminated in open rebellion, but after Yamato troops killed him in 528 it was possible to pursue the government's anti-Silla policy with renewed resolution. Following Iwai's demise, the Chikugo Plain in north Kyushu was prepared as a staging area for further attacks against Silla. Nevertheless, the policy failed and Japan was forced to fall back on its own defences and eventually felt the need to reinforce these when the alliance with Paekche later collapsed.

These so-called 'mountain castles' consist of long walls ten m. or more in height located on hill tops that rise 200 to 300 m. above the plain. The area enclosed would provide protection for substantial communities who might wish to reside within or in the neighbourhood.

The highest walls are at Goshogatani and the finest workmanship is at   Plate 5
Zoyama in the squarish-cut stones in the walls. As exposed, these last
measure between 1 and 1.5 m. on a side.

These fortifications have two basic plans. One, the mountain castle,
takes the form of a continuous stone wall (or perhaps partly an earthen
wall), roughly fan-shaped, with a forward line set out on the plain. The
other, called *kōgoishi* (divine defences), is composed of walls in more or
less horseshoe-shape, cutting across valleys and including water control
devices. Both types have Korean counterparts, but the former is the
direct result of Paekche instructors supervising the work. The best   *Fig. 13*
examples of the former are Ōno-jō, Ki-jō and Ito-jō, and of the latter,
Zoyama, Kōrasan, Kagenoma and Goshogatani. Other, smaller   Plates 4, 5
fortifications could be listed.

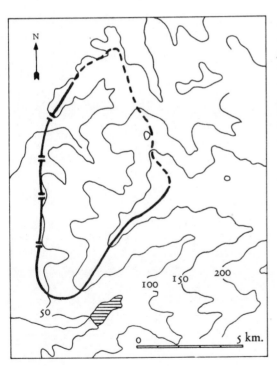

*Fig. 13   Plan of
Zoyama mountain
fortification, Setaka-
chō, Yamato county,
Fukuoka prefecture.
Four water sluices
were constructed on
the west side; sixth
century*

The stone wall at Ito-jō is about 3 m. in height. It runs along the plain in the shape of an arc, then turns back at either end to join at an acute angle on the hill behind. The positions of the watch towers and gates are marked by stone bases for wooden columns; the former were two by three bays in size. Grooves in the gate stones are slots for wooden doors.

Ōno-jō had a double line of defences on the western side consisting of an outer wall of stone and an inner bank of earth. The remains of more than 30 buildings were found at both Ōno-jō and Ki-jō, most of which were apparently storehouses if one may judge by the quantity of rice that was unearthed at the latter. Stone bases for the columns of many structures indicate standard sizes of five by three and four by three bays.

Plate 5

The horseshoe-shaped walls may extend as far as 3 km. Water gates with one or more sluices were built to control the flow of water through valleys, and both Zoyama and Kagenoma had wooden pipes laid below the surface. Zoyama has a stone structure that could have worked like a dam; it measures 7 m. across. A calculation is that it may have backed up a small lake about 1 km. square.[3] A water pipe found there has a diameter of 1.5 m.

NORTHERN FORTIFICATIONS

Fig. 14

With the prospects dimmed for foreign expansion in the south, the government took another look at its northern flank and began to open up coastal roads and river passes, extending its land control measures and looking for more opportunities to acquire gold. The result was a prolonged war against the Ezo (or Emishi), the local inhabitants of the Tōhoku region. These people are generally regarded as early Ainu, the ancestors of the present people who live in parts of Hokkaido. They were well entrenched in north Honshu and were able to hold off the best troops the Japanese could muster for over a century after this policy was put into effect.

Reports on skirmishes with the Ezo go back well into the Tomb period, at which time these people were described in Chinese fashion as being totally barbaric and lacking any redeeming virtues. Pockets of Ezo still existed on the western side at the time of the Taika Reform, but contact with them was not disruptive until the government started to apply pressure in the eighth century.

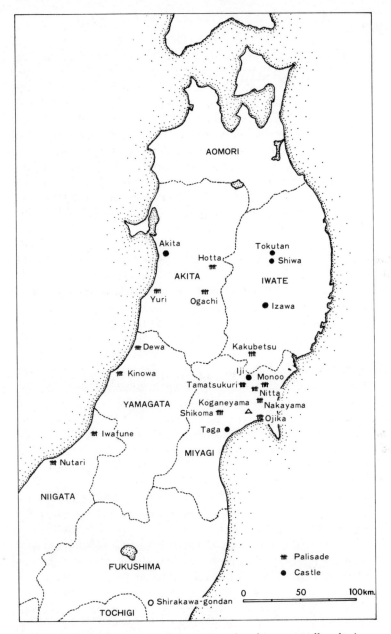

Fig. 14 Early fortifications in north Japan. Several castles were initially palisades

The literature dealing with the northern campaigns begins to include more frequent references to fights with the Ezo and the construction of *saku* (palisades, or perhaps stockades) after the foundation of the Heijō capital. The 'pacification' policy was being implemented from that vantage point. The famous Dewa stockade is noted for the first time in the records of 711, and its shifted location is a simple gauge of territorial acquisition by the Japanese. At that time it was situated near the west coast, along the Mogami River, in what is now Yamagata prefecture; by 733 it had been moved north to Akita. When Taga-jō, the Dazaifu of the north, was built a little later, several other stockades also went up. Such elaborate preparations were the signal for all out efforts to bring the Ezo to heel.

Writers of that time made no effort to conceal the humiliating losses by itemizing the combat casualties of numerous engagements throughout the earlier half of the century, and a revolt in 774 and consistent Ezo victories in the following years forced the court to devote full attention to the problem.

Stock-piling went on for a number of years as weapons and provisions were stored at Taga-jō and reinforcements were sent in, yet 789 was still a year of serious reverses and it was not until 794 that the first significant victory was won and not until Sakanoue Tamuramaro was appointed general in charge of northern troops in 797 that the court received consistent reports of steady and lasting successes. In a spectacular career of a few short years, Sakanoue Tamuramaro defeated the Ezo and built Izawa-jō and Shiwa-jō. In territorial terms the Japanese had actually taken the most land between 750 and 780, but as the Ezo withdrew and their domain shrank, their resistance stiffened and the Japanese were forced into more bitter fighting.

While an epitaph says that Taga-jō was built in 724 by General Ōno Azumabito, the most acceptable date is around 737. The Shoku Nihongi speaks of Taga-saku (palisade). In 780 it is called Taga-jō (castle). Taga-jō was the provincial capital and military headquarters of Mutsu and remained the provincial capital in the ninth century, but the army base was transferred to Izawa-jō (Misawa city, Iwate prefecture) in 804, to a more northerly point in closer touch with the enemy.

Taga-jō is on the summit of a hill about 30 m. higher than the surrounding land. It was encircled by earthworks outlining an area 10 chō

(1000 m.) north-south by 8 chō (800 m.) east-west. Within the rectangle was a smaller central fortification of which ramparts still remain. Tiles have been found at many places on the site, and a central building on a platform, undoubtedly the chief office, had base stones for columns.

The temple is located in the south-eastern part of the citadel. Parts of it have been excavated in recent years. It had a rectangular earthen wall and the usual complement of buildings. The pagoda was probably three stories high, to judge by the 21-ft span of the first roof and the size of the metal rings of the spire which were recovered. Its columns stood on natural stone bases. The Lecture Hall was much larger than the Main Hall. An eight by four bay building, it measured 89 by 47 ft, but was considerably reduced in size when rebuilt after a fire. Finds of Sue and Haji pottery tend to set the earlier date for the fortification, while some pieces of Sanage pottery recovered from the pagoda site range from the ninth to the eleventh centuries.

The similarity between roof tiles found here and at the fortifications of Shikoma, Nitta and Tamatsukuri, all in Miyagi prefecture, implies that the four were contemporary[4] and is corroborative evidence for the dates of at least three of the fortifications said to have been built at the same time as Taga-jō.

The fortifications of the north differed diametrically from those in the south in both the way they related to the terrain and in the materials used, with only minor exceptions. Except for Momo-jō, most were built on a plain. Taga-jō, Akita-jō and the Tamatsukuri palisade were constructed on quite low hills. Such fortifications were surrounded by wooden fences, although parts of stone walls are preserved at Hotta and Iwafune. Earthen banks and dry moats were frequently added, the former already a recognized feature in the south.

Several of the strategically located palisades, erected in the north for the stationing of troops in the war against the Ezo, were converted to castles (*jō*) in developments which were directly connected with the progress of the war, the increase of garrisons and the disposition of troops.

Many of these stockades appear by name in the old records, but there are two good archaeological sites for which no references have been found: Kinowa in Yamagata prefecture and Hotta in Akita prefecture. Kinowa yielded Nara period tiles. A guess is that a wooden fence, 3 m. high in places, ran for 3 km. at both places.[5] The periphery of the regular

Fig. 15

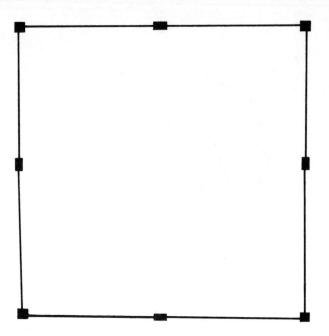

Fig. 15   Plans of northern palisades of (left) Kinowa, Sakata city, Yamagata pre- fecture; and (right) Hotta, Senboku village, Senboku county, Akita prefecture; second half of seventh century

plan at Hotta is 1,350 m. east-west and 720 m. north-south. Its four gates each had eight columns. Kinowa is the only one with watch towers at the four corners; each was 2 by 3 bays. The gates varied in size, the south gate being the largest. The number of buildings has not been determined. The closely-spaced fence posts were square in section, and ranged from 20 to 30 cm. a side. A partially decipherable inscription on a wooden tally from Hotta refers to the 26th day of an intercalary 4th month. The only reasonable possibilities are the years 760, 817, 855 and 874. Whichever it may be, the stockade was apparently used in the late Nara or the early Heian period, or probably in both.[6]

Other fortifications in the Tōhoku include Izawa-jō and Akita-jō. The latter, at Terauchi-chō in Akita prefecture, at the mouth of the Omono River, was constructed between 734 and 736. Four years of excavations starting in 1959 showed a rather similar inner fortification to that at Taga-jō, fenced in, and containing storehouses in its western sector. Outside, to the south-east, lay a Main Hall, a Lecture Hall and a sūtra repository. All were within a perimeter measuring 1.3 by 1 km.[7]

The 878 destruction of Akita-jō by the Ezo in their final assault accounted for the loss of 161 office buildings, the capture of 1500 horses,

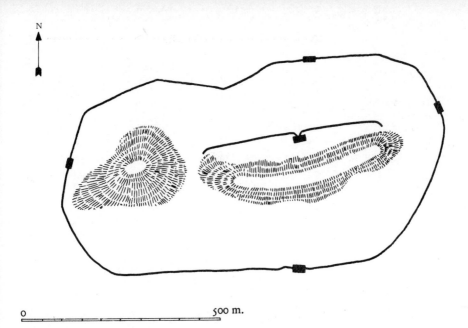

N

0   500 m.

300 helmets and suits of armour, rice and other items. Little was done to rebuild Akita⁄jō, but the Ezo had expended themselves and the Japanese northern fortifications had served out their purpose.

For their part, the Ezo built *chashi* (called *tate* by the Japanese), earthworks of a defensive nature, to withstand the Japanese encroach⁄ment on their territory. Square and rectangular pit⁄dwellings have been found on the slopes of hills and near the ends of plateaus in the neigh⁄bourhood of these earthworks. Like many early historic pits of houses, they contain a central fireplace and an oven built against a wall. Corroded iron ingots and iron tools, Sue pottery, and beads of glass and agate are relatively common relics, and rice grains on the bottoms of vessels show that the Ezo practised agriculture—that is, assuming that trade in rice with the Japanese could not possibly have provided for all of the needs of so thoroughly settled a people.

The description of the Ezo in the Nihon Shoki runs as follows: they have no sexual restrictions; they drink blood and wear furs; they live in holes in the winter and in trees in the summer; they show no gratitude, only revenge; there is no personal honour or integrity even among relatives; they are as fast as animals and climb mountains with the speed of birds; they may live on pillaging and flee by disappearing into the forests and mountains; in short, civilization never touched them.[8] Judging by their remains, however, they were obviously far more civilized than they were given credit for[9] and their utensils and domestic equipment at least were not unlike those used by the Japanese. Official wars or not, there must have been substantial trade passing between the two peoples, or one is at a loss to account for what appears to have been a roughly equal standard of living on both sides of the lines.

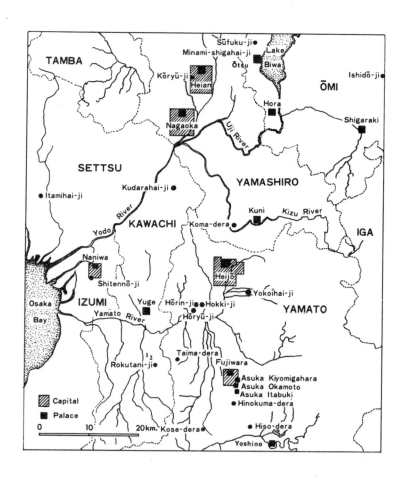

CHAPTER VI

Palaces

The early capitals in Japan were always identified with the residence of
the emperor. Even the first formal city was only an adjunct to the palace;
it was called at first *shinyaku-kyō*: new expanded palace. Each emperor
built his own palace, avoiding the place where his predecessor had died.
Family connections, resulting from consorts raising not a few offspring
of rulers away from the palace, encouraged a newly selected emperor to
live in the vicinity of his mother's home. The flimsy nature of the
architecture often made it better to build anew than to repair, applying
the lessons learned at the Ise shrines, where periodic rebuilding in the
guise of ritual has been, in fact, a practical necessity.

Fig. 16

As the base of central authority was enlarged, frequent moving
became increasingly less practical, but even as eighth century rulers were
residing in 'permanent' palaces in Heijō they were constantly erecting
palaces in other places. Total resignation to the use of a single palace
came only after the emperor had become a powerless figurehead in
Kyoto and found himself in no position to act independently.

The immediate predecessors of Empress Suiko lived at several places:
near Sakurai along the northern edge of the Asuka region and at
Kashiwara. Suiko herself was at Toyura and Owarida. Suiko's
successor, Jomei, indulged in the luxury of four palaces, perhaps, as the
literature occasionally infers when rationalizing such mobility, with the
noble intention of being near his people. Kōtoku lived at Naniwa
(Osaka), and Tenchi near Lake Biwa, but Temmu built traditionally
in Asuka. Jitō and two successors used the new Fujiwara capital.

Fig. 26

Seven rulers built over seven decades of administration at Heijō, but
three of these also built elsewhere: Shōmu at Kuni, Shigaraki and
Naniwa; Junnin at Hora, and Shōtoku at Yuge. Changes were
motivated by political reasons and much stock was put in omens and
the auspiciousness of a site. Calamities or a series of near calamities were
signals to move.

In contrast to the temples, which were the symbols of the transcen-
dental in the Buddhist view and thus the permanent, all of the early

*Fig. 16   Palaces and capitals in the Home Provinces and major early temples outside
the Asuka region (Fig. 26). Numbers 1 and 2 mark the tombs of Prince Shōtoku and
Empress Suiko*

palaces, including the one in Kyoto, have been destroyed. Palaces are known only through archaeological investigations and scattered references in old texts, and the earliest painting to show a palace is a later copy of a twelfth century scroll.

Palace archaeology started around 1934 when the northern half of Asuka was investigated for the location of the Fujiwara palace. Palaces before Fujiwara lacked tile roofs and stone bases for columns often leaving little for the archaeologist to find if stone paved floors did not exist.

IKARUGA PALACE

The earliest palace site now identified is the retreat-palace constructed by Prince Shōtoku at Ikaruga. Begun in 601, it stood on the spot occupied since the eighth century by the Tō-in of the Hōryū-ji, in a quiet place well north of the Asuka area. The prince built a temple nearby in 607 which, according to some records, was lost in a fire in 670. The palace was destroyed during the feuds of 643, over twenty years after his death.

Fig. 17

The results of the 1939 excavations were informative insofar as they showed the presence of much burnt earth, a well and numerous pillar holes. Two rather large rectangular buildings had their longest dimensions running north and south, while a third ran east and west. This last one may have been connected with one of the others by a colonnade, and there are also parts of smaller buildings. If these are some of its main buildings, together they do not appear to constitute a standard palace plan. They are closer to a *shinden-zukuri* scheme,[1] that is to say, a Chinese-originated arrangement of buildings with associated garden, but it was a style not well known in Japan until it was widely adopted by aristocratic families in the later Heian period.

ASUKA PALACES

In the south of Asuka and east of the river is situated the remains of what is believed by many to be the Asuka Itabuki Palace. It was dug after 1960 by the Kashiwara Archaeological Institute and parts of it are left exposed today. If its identification is correct—it is cautiously called merely Asuka-kyō (Asuka capital) by those who await proof—this is the palace that was ready for occupancy by Empress Kōgyoku in 642. She was the first woman to take the throne twice, which she did after an interval of a decade. Known as Empress Saimei for the second reign,

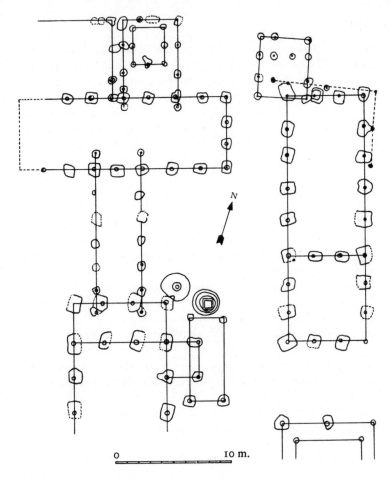

Fig. 17 Plan of excavated part of Ikaruga Palace of Prince Shōtoku, under Tō-in, Hōryū-ji, Ikaruga-machi, Ikoma county, Nara prefecture. Early seventh century

she used either the same palace or the same spot until the buildings were burnt to the ground, after which she lived at Kawahara.

The remains include substantial stone-floored areas and buildings, remnants of wooden pillars in place, and a large well which still works today. However, it has not been possible to correspond these features

Plate 9

satisfactorily with the literature. The Nihon Shoki speaks of the twelve gates of the Itabuki Palace being guarded, and refers to its Adminis-tration Palace (Chōdō-in) and Imperial Council Hall (Daigoku-den). These have not been identified. Perhaps the writers of the eighth century literature used current terms for parts of buildings not yet standardized in the seventh century.

Itabuki is literally 'board-covered'[2]: understandably, therefore, no tiles have been found. Itabuki was the scene of the assassination of Soga no Iruka in 644, the head of the Soga family, and the destruction of the palace took place in 655, within a year after Empress Saimei had occupied the throne.

The temporary nature of the palaces inhibited the use of permanent materials, but advanced features, already known in temple architecture, began to creep in slowly. These would include stone floors, stone bases for pillars, tile roofs replacing thatch, cloisters instead of surrounding fences or walls and, not the least, formal grouping of buildings. Empress Saimei intended to roof a palace under construction at Owarida with tiles. It was impossible to do so because too many projects left each with insufficient manpower, and it fell to the lot of Empress Jitō or one of her followers to put tiles on the palace at Fujiwara in 694 or later. The Itabuki Palace was lost the same winter that the Owarida project was abandoned, and Saimei moved into the Kawahara Palace,[3] a palace that is little known through either the literature or its archaeology. When the temple called Kawahara-dera was excavated, an underground drainage system was discovered which is believed to have been con-nected with the palace.

Larger palaces were built following the Taika Reform (645–46). The old texts are much more thorough in their references to the Asuka Kiyomigahara, the palace built by Emperor Temmu in 672, which lay *Fig. 26* north of the Asuka-dera. According to the Nihon Shoki, it was situated south of the palace of Okamoto,[4] but this may be inaccurate. The Nihon Shoki recounts a reign full of receptions and entertainment; many parts of the palace are mentioned, leading one to assume that this was the first complete palace in Japan, provided with all the proper formal features. Archaeology has furnished a minimum of information: we know only that the supposed site had stone sculptures and stone pavements.

In a fully developed palace a sequence of units followed each other from
south to north: (1) a forecourt with a pair of buildings facing each other,
called Chōshū-den—Imperial Assembly Hall (since none of these terms
translate adequately, rough but workable approximations in the tradition
started by others will have to do); (2) a main court with four or more
(usually twelve) rectangular buildings, called Chōdō-in—Administration Palace; four were lined up on either side, also facing each other,
additional ones at the south end; (3) a smaller courtyard on the north
enclosing one or more buildings, called the Daigoku-den—Imperial
Council Hall; and (4) a small additional complex outside the cloistered
area known as the Dairi—Imperial Residence. This last part is assumed
to have existed at Fujiwara⁵ and its presence has been determined for the
Naniwa and Heijō palaces.

Figs 18, 19, 22

The Imperial Assembly Hall was a gathering place entered through a
gate that sometimes had a kind of portico. It led into the large area which,
although separated by walls or cloisters, formed one unit with the
Imperial Council Hall, and which, together, are known as the
Administration Palace. Each hall in the main courtyard was a chōdō.
The eight side-buildings in a fully developed palace were the headquarters of the Eight Ministries. The courtyard served for various
installations, official annual ceremonies, unusual court functions and a
few receptions. Four more buildings were squeezed into the southern
end of this courtyard in the Fujiwara, early Naniwa and Heijō palaces.
On the basis of archaeological information, the Fujiwara Palace was the
first to have had a full complement of buildings in this section. The
buildings were smaller and the block was less crowded in the Naniwa
Palace.

The Imperial Council Hall constituted the holy of holies which, by
the time of the Heijō Palace, had acquired extra status through the
elevation of the entire unit on a terrace above the level of the twelve halls.
The space of this area tended to be reduced in successive palaces, although
its main, south-oriented building was increased in size. For example,
this structure was normally four bays deep, but it had seven southern bays
in the Fujiwara Palace, nine in the Heijō Palace and eleven in the Heian
Palace. Credit for this consistent enlargement is given to the heightened
prestige of the emperor.⁶

Fig. 19

Early Buddhist Japan

FUJIWARA PALACE

Fig. 18

In a decade of excavation that began about 1934 and was resumed in 1966 for two years when a highway bypass was started, much of the east side of the Fujiwara Palace has been unearthed. Rows of post-holes mark the periphery of the palace on its north, east and west sides, and a wide moat lay 18 m. outside this fence. A cloister, colonnaded both inside and out, surrounded the central court and part of the rear court; the northern half of this rear court was finished with a simple cloister. The forecourt was enclosed by an earthen wall. The two northernmost buildings in the Administration Palace were nine by four bays and were therefore six bays shorter than the buildings along the sides, and three bays shorter than the pairs of buildings at the end. All were four bays deep. Gateways may have existed on either side of the central block (despite the reconstruction by Kudō) to judge by some irregularity of the pillar holes. Base stones have been found for the interior wooden columns of the twelve halls, leading to the view that they all had raised wooden floors.[7] Chairs were probably used on dirt floors of the later Heijō and Heian palaces, following a practice introduced from China.[8].

The Imperial Council Hall building is off-centre; the alignment of the side buildings leaves something to be desired, and the cloister of the rear court extends asymmetrically from the two side-buildings which here, incidentally, acted as gates. All of these are minor aberrations that must have occurred as a full palace complex matured.

There is no agreement on the size of the city of Fujiwara. One sug-gestion is for measurements of 2.6 by 1.7 km. north-south and east-west respectively, with a population ranging between 30,000 and 40,000.[9] Another is for a size about 3 by 2 km.[10] These estimates may be compared with Heijō (Nara) and Heian (Kyoto) as 4.5 by 4 and 5.4 by 4.5 km. respectively.

Existing major Yamato roads may have been used as the natural borders of the Fujiwara capital on the north, east and west sides.[11] The distance between these roads from east to west is an even four ri, about 2.1 km. According to Kishi, the available space was simply divided into squares to make eight east-west units and twelve north-south units. The ancient literature mentions twelve block chiefs. This means, however, that the southernmost line of blocks would be cut through by an old road traversing hilly ground that already had temples built along

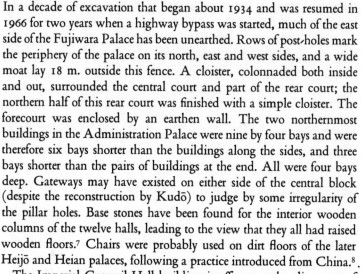

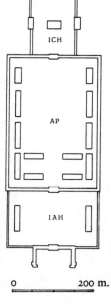

ICH

AP

IAH

0   200 m.

Fig. 18 Plan of the Fujiwara Palace, Kashiwara city (jurisdictional area), Nara prefecture, built by Empress Jitō. 694–710

66

it. Perhaps this block was never completed, but by such calculations the Asuka River would pass just beyond the corner of the palace as it flowed through the city diagonally.

Fig. 26

In the calculations suggested above, two of the great temples of the time, the Daikandai-ji and the early Yakushi-ji, fit into the blocks ideally. The fact that they conform so well leaves little doubt about their connection with the planning of the capital. The Daikandai-ji appears frequently in the records after 682; the Yakushi-ji would have been finished by the end of the century, if not a little earlier. With this in mind Kishi must be correct when he says that when Temmu decided on a site for a palace at the time of a visit to the 'capital' on the 9th day of the 3rd month in his 13th year (684), he had actually selected the Fujiwara site.[12] The Nihon Shoki fails to mention the name of the site, and Temmu died before any moves took place. So the Yakushi-ji and the huge Daikandai-ji, the latter on the drawing boards as early as 673 and already a major landmark, were pivotal points when the city was being laid out. Incidentally, the Daikandai-ji was moved to the same relative position in the Heijō capital when transfers were later in order.

To crown the argument that Temmu was responsible for the plan of Fujiwara, Kishi reasons that Temmu's tomb, built in the first and second years of Jitō's reign (687–88), is on a direct line with the southern extension of Fujiwara's main street. This would be no coincidence. Given the custom of the ruler selecting the spot for his tomb and supervising its erection during his lifetime, Temmu, in effect, composed a mandala, a Buddhist magical relationship, into which, later, went the ashes of Jitō.

Plate 64

HEIJŌ PALACE AND CAPITAL

Fujiwara was almost entirely abandoned when the capital was moved to Heijō. The promulgation of the Taihō Civil and Penal Codes at the beginning of the eighth century undoubtedly stimulated fresh interest in a new bureaucratic structure modelled along Chinese lines. A move would make it easier to proceed with appointments. Each successive capital was also a further effort to accommodate the expanding bureau-cratic system and to find a more convenient location for the natural lines of traffic to reach the city from the provinces.

In 707 the officials were asked to give consideration to the transfer, which had been suggested by Emperor Mommu. He died prematurely in the same year at the age of 25 and left the actual business of the change to his mother, Empress Gemmyō, who performed a holding operation until her seven-year-old son, later Emperor Shōmu, could take over. Divination processes were put into action to determine the propitiousness of the site, and construction was far enough along for the transfer to be carried out in 710.

Fig. 9

Many tumuli lay in the way of the workmen clearing the land in the north of the Yamato region for the city of Heijō. Two large keyhole-shaped tombs had to be totally or partially levelled to make space for the palace, and there were probably smaller ones. The tomb attributed to Emperor Heijō (*d.* 824) is the knoll of a fifth century keyhole-shaped tumulus, the southern half of which must have been destroyed at this time. There are several large, moated tombs just to the north of the old city. Tampering with old tombs brought on pangs of official conscience, however, and the supervisor of palace construction received an order on the 16th day of the 11th month, 709, to restore to their original condition any tombs that had been disturbed by this work, although how this was to have been done for tumuli is not suggested. The Imperial Residence stands on the spot occupied by a keyhole-shaped tomb that was moated on the south side. Many of the wooden grave-goods removed from its chamber were thrown into a neighbouring ditch, but the metal grave-goods were fair game at the time. Perhaps this area, with its many tombs, could have been avoided, but an old Yamato road, the one running along the west side of the Fujiwara capital, was to be used for the main street of Heijō.

One can be grateful for the historical circumstances that saved the remains of the old capital of Heijō for posterity. It was the capital for seventy-four years, but, unlike Kyoto, its legacy is an array of temples which were relatively unimportant as military targets in medieval wars but of supreme importance as objects of endless pilgrimages that still go on today. The temples preserved the religious art, the Shōsōin preserved the court art, while the daily and secular arts, preserved in the earth, are now being revealed through archaeology, thanks to the fact that the city moved east and the old palace area and western part of the city went to seed, reverting to rice-fields.

The site is within the jurisdiction of Nara city today, but lies well west of the heavily populated areas. In fact, it is about 6 km. from the centre of modern Nara, which is now situated on the eastern edge of the old capital. Most of the land is owned by the Kinki Nippon Railway, whose president generously donated a large tract for a five year excavation. The results were so promising that the project was extended another five and then designated a continuing excavation for thirty or more years, conducted under the auspices of the Commission for the Protection of Cultural Properties of Nara Prefecture.

Plate 21

Excavations at Heijō actually started as early as 1924. Shortly after-wards it became apparent that two similar if not identical complexes of buildings lay side by side, not unlike the arrangement of the shrines at Ise. This is now an accepted fact, and it may be that archaeological work has been concentrating on the secondary palace [13] with the primary one to the west yet to be dug. It might then be conjectured that the emperor had an alternate set of buildings available and even at Heijō was not obliged to live in the residence occupied by his predecessor. The life span of the buildings was never much longer than an average reign.

Fig. 19

That the area was settled as far back as the Yayoi period is proved by the remains of a large village under the south-west sector of the east palace. The tumuli are adequate evidence for its use during the Tomb period. Documents leave little doubt that the emperors generally preferred it to other locations throughout the eighth century and, even after Heian was built (794), attempts were made to restore the capital to Heijō. Con-tinuous reconstruction over the same spots in the Heijō Palace has showed up in successive stratigraphic layers. The kitchen area of the palace was still in use toward the end of the eighth century if the recovery of one coin of the Ryūhei-eihō series, issued in 796, can be regarded as sufficient proof.

The Heijō Palace may have been the first to have had a complete, fully enclosed Imperial Residence at the northern end with a large, U-shaped courtyard behind the buildings. Shōmu apparently built a rather similar complex at Naniwa. The main Imperial Residence hall was nine bays long by five deep, each bay measuring 10 ft in length. The enclosing cloister is recognized by the presence of its post-holes.

Stone bases for columns were still normally not in use in palaces, but by piecing together information from the size of post-holes, inter-columniation, presence or absence of tiles, raised platforms for buildings,

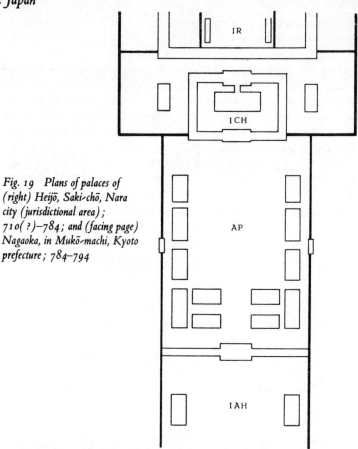

IR

ICH

Fig. 19   Plans of palaces of
(right) Heijō, Saki-chō, Nara
city (jurisdictional area);
710(?)–784; and (facing page)
Nagaoka, in Mukō-machi, Kyoto
prefecture; 784–794

AP

IAH

a building's surrounding rainwater pebble trough (which tells the precise extent of overhang of an eave), it can be determined whether the building was of the heavy, 'temple' style of construction or the light-weight, 'palace' style. From these details, therefore, one knows whether it had a tile roof and, more than likely, the accompanying hip-gable construction or a thatched roof with the simpler, gable construction.

The platform of the Sujaku (or Shujaku, Red Sparrow) Gate has been found. This was a typically named gate associated with the tutelary spirit of the south in the Chinese concept, the Red Bird, the middle one of three gates leading into the palace precinct. The gate was of tremendous size, even larger than the present well-known South Great Gate (Nandai-mon) of the Tōdai-ji. Built with two tile roofs, the upper one in the hipped-gable style, this five by two bay structure probably stood on stone bases, had a wall running laterally throughout, and the usual three openings. The structural system would have compared favourably with that of the Tōshōdai-ji's Main Hall. The woodwork was painted red and the mud-plaster walls white.

The recovery of almost 20,000 wooden tallies[14] in recent years from rubbish pits, ditches, rainwater drains and a well in the Heijō Palace has furnished much information on the taxes received at the court. Enough writing is legible on about 120 of these to tell the full story of what goods came in from which provinces and when. The tallies range

Plate 11

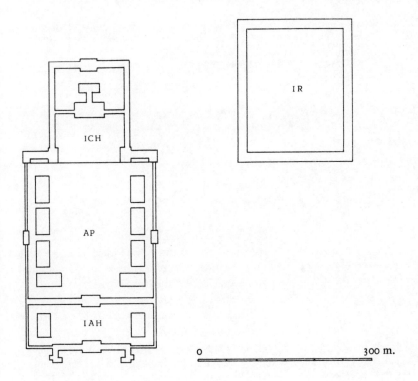

0   300 m.

Plates 14–16

between 10 and 50 cm. in length. The earliest is dated to 709, the latest to 782, and business was at its best around 745–46 if the number of dated tallies is any indication. The dates are given only in era names (*nengō*), the use of which was ordered in the Taihō Civil and Penal codes to replace the earlier sixty-year cyclical system introduced in 604. A small number of tallies has been found at the Fujiwara Palace; they carry dates in both the older and newer systems, and so fit into the change-over stage. It took the discovery of these tallies at Fujiwara in the 1966–68 excavations to convince the few remaining sceptics that the site was in fact the actual location of the Fujiwara Palace.

Fig. 20

Wooden tallies were also markers for internal communications within the palace itself at Heijō, recording the distribution and inventory of commodities. Most rice and *mugi* (closely akin to barley) came from the periphery of the Home Provinces. Salt was sent in from the Fukui coast due north of Nara, the Wakayama coast on the western side of the Kii

Fig. 20   Taxes sent to the Heijō Palace for its support in the eighth century, according to information on the wooden tallies found at the palace

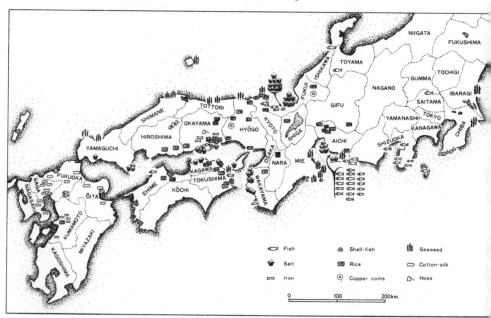

72

Peninsula, and north-east Shikoku. Cotton-silk was shipped up exclusively from north Kyushu. Seaweed was brought in from the north Chūgoku coastal areas and some arrived from the east side of the Kii Peninsula. Fish, such as mackerel, tuna, salmon, shark and *ayu* (a kind of trout), along with freshwater crayfish, came in quantity from the Atsumi Bay area of Aichi prefecture and, to a lesser extent, from the Izu Peninsula, Shizuoka. It was dried or salted. Shell-fish, such as abalone and mussels, were sent in from many points but in particular from the Bōsō Peninsula of Chiba prefecture. Each area was transmitting its speciality, and the people of the eastern Inland Sea had little choice but to provide the greatest support for the capital. Iron ore arrived from Okayama prefecture. Manufactured products were few, but coins were received from Fukui and Hyōgo and iron blades of a kind of draw hoe (*suki*) from inland points in Okayama and Hiroshima prefectures.

By and large, most of the commodities originated in outlying areas of the Kansai, in the most highly developed region organizationally and commercially, the most convenient for the rapid transport of perishable goods and, not the least, the region the most subject to direct pressure from the capital. The Yamato Plain itself contributed surprisingly little, but much of its resident labour force was perpetually siphoned off by demands from the capital and no small amount of its land was already producing regular donations of crops towards the upkeep of temples.

A surprising number of wooden articles, consisting of utensils, tools, containers, fans, combs, human figures and even a shield, have been found, mostly from the usual eighth century disposal system—drains and ditches along the outer walls of the palace precincts. Much pottery has also been unearthed, including sets composed of plates, dishes and stands. The pottery is chiefly the domestic, reddish Haji and the finer, greyish Sue ware. Rather rare is the recovery of any other type, but a small amount of coloured glazed pieces modelled after the T'ang Chinese Three-colour ware has appeared. Most is quite fragmentary, but there is one rather large vase (39.2 cm.) in two colours that doubtless made a very distinguished ornament in the palace.

About 150 pottery 'ink-stones' have been dug up at the palace, largely of Sue ware. They are occasionally accompanied by water droppers. Since ordinary people used the lids of pots, these can be taken as belonging to a court style. They are mostly round and are provided

Plates 18, 19

Plate 17

Fig. 21

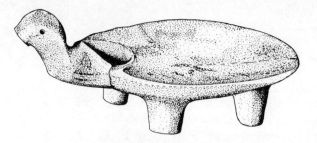

Fig. 21   Pottery 'ink-stone'
with animal's head, found in
Heijō Palace, perhaps made at
a Sanage kiln. Length 16.5 cm.
Eighth century

with legs. More decorative ones, for instance with animal features, were made in the earlier half of the eighth century, but have been found only at Heijō, Dazaifu and where they were produced in Aichi prefecture. The simpler round ones, in style by the latter half of the century, are distributed the length of the country.

NANIWA PALACE

The Naniwa Palace remains are locked within heavy concentrations of modern buildings of Osaka city, in Hōenzaka-chō, a situation that has considerably circumscribed the effectiveness of excavations. The palaces are identified with emperors Temmu and Shōmu of the seventh and eighth centuries, but the spot or area had probably been used by such fifth century rulers as Ōjin, Nintoku and Richū of the 'Naniwa dynasty', and the construction of the sixteenth century castle near the confluence of the rivers just north of the palace site points up later recognition of the advantages of the location and marks the start of Osaka as a commercial city.

Some kind of regal headquarters existed at Naniwa in the Asuka period as early as 583, but during the reign of Kōgyoku the capital is said to have been moved there and her successor, Kōtoku, spent most of his reign at Naniwa. The Nagara Toyosaki Palace was built at this time. Empress Saimei lived at Naniwa for a short period around 660, so one is easily led to think that a royal residence was usually available at Naniwa long before Emperor Temmu built the 'first' palace in the seventh year of his reign (679).[15] There is rather little evidence, however, to show that he occupied it for any length of time, if at all.

Fig. 22

The preserved parts of the Nagara Toyosaki and Temmu's palaces parallel very closely sections of Shōmu's palace. Temmu may have built around an existing nucleus, but it still seems only fair to his place in history to credit him with the first genuinely formal plan at Naniwa.

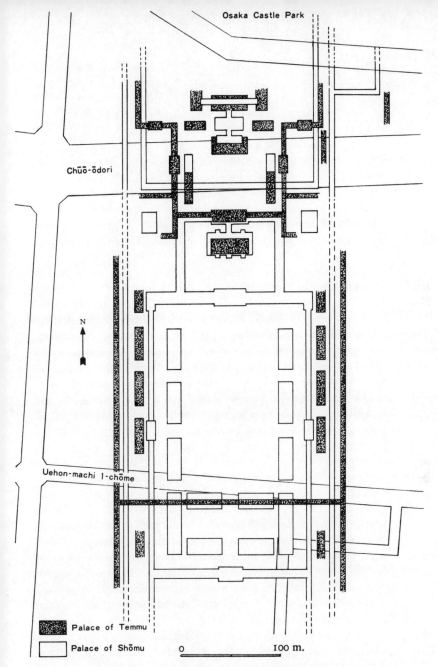

Osaka Castle Park

Chūō-ōdori

N

Uehon-machi 1-chōme

Palace of Temmu

Palace of Shōmu

0   100 m.

Fig. 22 Plans of palaces of Emperor Temmu and Emperor Shōmu at Naniwa, in Hōenzaka-chō, Higashi ward, Osaka city. Seventh and eighth centuries

75

There are no tiles for this period—the roofs were of thatch—and no base stones. According to the records, all but the arsenal went up in a spectacular conflagration in 686. Charred remains of posts in holes give proof to the end of this phase.[16]

This opened the door for Empress Jitō, the distinguished architect of Fujiwara, to embark on the next phase of building at Naniwa. Taking into consideration all she had invested in Fujiwara, the Naniwa project may seem rather extravagant, but it is relatively clear that Naniwa was only secondary, as was so often the case with 'detached' palaces.[17] Emperor Mommu used it; so did Empress Genshō, but it was Shōmu who started to build it up to major proportions soon after ascending the throne in 724. He was no less prodigal; he was building almost simul-taneously at Heijō and elsewhere. This palace may then have been kept habitable until the last decade of the eighth century; later relics found on the site are tiles of the Edo period (after the seventeenth century).

Shōmu's palace overlay the earlier remains almost exactly. The north-south orientation is identical and rows of columns and walls ran alongside the older palace lines. The flanking buildings may have been outside the cloister of the Imperial Council Hall, and a full Imperial Residence was included in a separate enclosed area to the north.

The main roofs of the Naniwa Palace were tiled, but base stones were nowhere to be seen. The round end tiles are decorated with an eight-petalled lotus flower and a less usual series of concentric circles. The pantiles bear floral and parallel groove patterns, in typical eighth century style.

NAGAOKA AND HEIAN CAPITALS AND PALACES

The palace of the capital city of Nagaoka is in modern Mukō-machi in Otokuni county, Kyoto prefecture. Identification of the Nagaoka site came quite late. It has been investigated several times since 1955 when new construction in the area has necessitated rescue excavation or patches of land have otherwise been opened up for investigation. Today the area consists largely of clustered middle class residences, many of which have a little adjoining land for farming. A small park preserves a section of the palace outlines for public inspection.

Plate 20

It is not explained why a transfer of the capital had to be engineered so suddenly,[18] but officials were appointed in charge of the building of the

Nagaoka Palace and associated capital on the 1st day of the 7th month in 784 and Emperor Kammu and his court moved in on the 27th day of the 12th month of the same year. In a six-month burst of activity, roughly 300,000 people were thrown into the project, while provinces forwarded their annual tribute directly to Nagaoka.

The Nagaoka move was the first public sign of Kammu's fight with the Heijō priests, but it also had much to do with manoeuvring between families. In this respect, the empresses played powerful roles, and one might remember that of the nine rulers whose dates span this time period, four were empresses. For an ambitious family, the ideal was to have the palace in its own stronghold; this situation was often coupled with arrangements whereby daughters were married into the royal family; hopefully, some would become consorts and one the empress. Shōmu had moved to Kuni and Naniwa because of just such family squabbles, in that case with the Tachibana and the ubiquitous Fujiwara.

The move to Nagaoka was spearheaded by Fujiwara Tanetsugu and was designed to situate the capital in more favourable Fujiwara-influenced territory. But Nagaoka lost its champion in about a year after its occupation when Tanetsugu was murdered by the crown prince while the emperor was in Nara. The site was certainly not a good choice, and it was not long before the spectre of Tanetsugu's death hung over it. Neither was it opportune that his killer, Prince Sawara, the emperor's younger brother who wanted the throne against Tanetsugu's wishes, died in exile. Despite Sawara's record as an assassin, the misfortunes and bad omens which harried Kammu were regarded as retribution by the dead prince, and efforts were made to placate his spirit, including the customary public prayers and offerings at shrines. He was reburied in a way befitting a prince and elevated posthumously to the rank of emperor. Leaving Nagaoka climaxed all efforts to appease his spirit. Most visitors who have seen both the site of Nagaoka and the city of Kyoto say their own private prayer of gratitude to Sawara, thankful that his spirit encouraged Kammu to give up Nagaoka in favour of Heian.

Emperor Kammu's running feud with the Heijō Buddhist priesthood is exemplified by the thirty or more orders he issued to temples,[19] requiring the priests to curb their rapacious ways, raise their moral standards and restrict the expansion of property and buildings. He was not anti-Buddhist as such; in time he pinned his hopes on new ideas being developed by Saichō (Dengyō Daishi), the priest who had studied in China and established the Tendai sect after his return to Japan. Kammu gave his personal support to Saichō's headquarters on Mt Hiei near Kyoto.

Fig. 19

Following a fairly standard plan, the Nagaoka palace was pro-portionally shorter than other palaces. The imperial quarters in the extreme north were apparently not isolated from the central unit by a full cloister but raised on a terrace so as to look down on the large courtyard below. The Imperial Residence was the model for the emperor's residence in the Heian Palace and consisted of one large building almost in the centre, a smaller seven by two bay building behind and probably connected to the former by a cloister, and a three by two bay gate in the north cloister.

The area of Nagaoka seems to have had no temples before the site was selected, and apparently attracted none during the ten years it was the capital. They may not have been officially banned, but it was made manifestly clear that they were not welcome.

The transfer to Heian was far less precipitate than the move to Nagaoka, yet almost as if by accident, while out hunting, Wake Kiyomaro noticed a good spot (doubtless he had been advised to be on the lookout for a new site) and the formalities were started in 793. The location was officially approved and tested against the philosophical principles, in this case, three mountains and two rivers, the local tutelary deities were notified of the impending move, the Sun Goddess at Ise was informed of the reasons for the change, and prayers were said at the tombs of emperors Tenchi and Kōnin. The 'tribes' were directed to build their gates, the land marked off, assignments made, the markets transferred and Emperor Kammu moved on the 18th day of the 11th month of 794. The fanfare speaks for wide popular support for the transfer, and it was not long before official signals went out that the site had more than met expectations. On the 4th day of the 12th month in the same year, a royal statement proclaimed the natural beauty of the area and the city was designated Heian-kyō, the Capital of Peace. Only a few frustrated emperors and Minamoto Yoritomo and his Hōjō suc-cessors of the Kamakura period ever questioned the wisdom of the choice of the site during the succeeding millenium that Kyoto served as the capital of Japan.

CHAPTER VII

Temples

The Japanese received the physical features of a temple from the Koreans, just as the Koreans had done from the Chinese before them. The Chinese had simply adapted their palace plan to the needs of a temple, and added a pagoda on the major axis. The temple was essentially built around this relic repository which grew out of the long tradition of the Indian *stūpa*. The Japanese for pagoda, *tō*, is an abbreviation for *sotōba*, a corruption of stūpa.

The entire group of temple buildings was surrounded by some kind of a wall, barrier or fence entered by way of at least one gate. Several eighth century Provincial Temples were enclosed by a mound and a moat.[1] The main entrance was the South Great Gate (*nandaimon*). Within this was a rectangular cloister with a south entrance known as the Middle Gate (*chūmon*); as the temple's nucleus, this cloistered area and its buildings are the *garan* (abbreviation of *sōgarama*, from the sanskrit *samgharama*). Near its centre stood the *kondō* (Golden Hall, hereafter Main Hall), and before it the pagoda. Behind the Main Hall was the Lecture Hall (*kōdō*) to which the cloister was often attached. Outside the cloister on either side stood a bell-tower (*shōrō*) and a sūtra repository (*kyōzō*), and still farther north a refectory (*jikidō*) flanked by living quarters (*sōbō*).

Only in the most unusual cases was there not a southern orientation, and after the Taika Reform the north-south axis rarely varied more than five degrees east of north.[2] Early Japanese temples were fairly standardized in size: small ones ordinarily occupied the equivalent of one chō square (about 2.45 acres) and large ones two chō square.

The ideal form of the early garans can be seen at the rebuilt Shitennō-ji in Osaka. This plan came from the Paekche kingdom of south-west Korea, known by the Japanese as Kudara. It is called the Kudara Style. Each building was placed on a longitudinal axis in a precise mathematical sequence. Measured from the centre of each building, the distances between the South Great Gate, Middle Gate, pagoda, Main Hall and Lecture Hall were in a ratio of 1.5:1:1:1.5 respectively. The pagoda's position was the most variable factor in temple planning.

Fig. 23

Plate 22

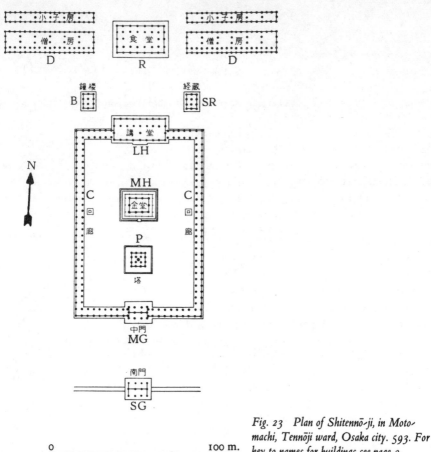

*Fig. 23   Plan of Shitennō-ji, in Moto-
machi, Tennōji ward, Osaka city. 593. For
key to names for buildings see page 9*

0   100 m.

While a single pagoda was present in the first century of temple construction and tended to dominate the forecourt, it changed in degree of
prominence and, by the Middle Asuka II (early Hakuhō) period in the
seventh century, was sometimes balanced off against other buildings.
Later, under Chinese influence, a pair of pagodas stood symmetrically
within the garan or had their own cloisters, in an arrangement that
became the standard plan of the early eighth century. Later in the eighth
century one pagoda was again the rule, placed off to one side. Relics
were buried under its centre pole, Buddhist images were placed to face

Plates 32,
33, 36, 37

80

the four cardinal directions on the ground floor level, and occasionally wall paintings decorated the interior walls of its first storey.

Pagodas normally had three bays on each side, requiring rows of four stones as supports for their wooden columns. There were four inner columns and a centre pole. Calculations made on the height of a pagoda to the width of its base have been useful in determining, for instance, whether the provinces actually erected the seven-storeyed pagodas they were ordered to construct by Emperor Shōmu. None of these stands today and no early paintings portray any, but the base stones for columns of pagodas are known at most of the Provincial Temple sites. The archae-ology of pagodas has benefited from the fact that the huge stones used to support the central pillar required so much manpower that once in place they were rarely ever moved again. By adapting information gathered from existing pagodas, recently destroyed examples and others known through texts, it has been calculated that the height of a pagoda is about forty times the diameter of the foot of its centre pole. Additionally, if the length of a side wall on the ground level ranges from nine to ten times the diameter of the centre pole, the pagoda was designed to have three storeys. By the same token, if it is seven to eight times it was to be a pagoda of five storeys, and if five to six times it was to be a pagoda of seven storeys.[3] In the case of the pagodas of the Provincial Temples it appears that the builders did in fact erect the seven-storeyed structures that were expected of them, suggesting even the possibility that they received fairly standard-ized building plans from the court's advisers on temple construction.

These temples are living entities today, but they will be described here as they were in early times. The Main Hall was the setting for major ceremonies. It enclosed the Buddha platform (*butsudan* or *sumidan*), a symbolic Mt Sumeru, on which the Buddha sat accompanied by a pair of bodhisattvas and protected by Four Heavenly Kings (*shi-tennō*) at the four corners. Other statues were often added, the walls were occasionally painted, metal ornaments and brocades were hung on the walls or columns, and one or more ornate canopies were suspended over the images.

Plates 44, 47

The platform occupied all or part of the space within an ambulatory. The latter allowed proper circumambulation for the pilgrim who would enter on the east side, pass the images on the south and move on clockwise to leave by the door through which he had come. Such

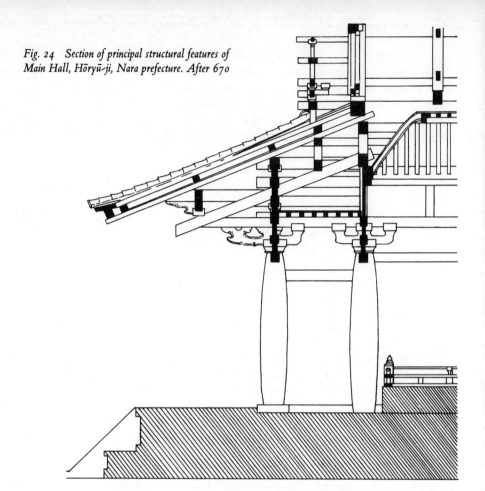

Fig. 24 *Section of principal structural features of Main Hall, Hōryū-ji, Nara prefecture. After 670*

Plates 27, 42   buildings had an odd number of bays on north and south. The central bays could be opened up as doors to allow light into the building, but at best the interior was subdued, the effect often sombre, in part due to the long overhang of the eaves. Outer bays had vertical wooden bars that acted as windows; these were closed by shutters.

Plate 48   The Lecture Hall, located at the rear of the cloistered area or behind, provided space for the monks to indulge in collective study. While often a larger building than the Main Hall, it was normally less complicated structurally. In this kind of architecture there was little adjustment to function. The size would vary, but otherwise the structural system was selected to stress the relative importance and position of the building.

The frequent earthquakes in Japan necessitated building in a minimum of solid materials save where they would be underfoot. Roof tiles were the chief exception. This resulted in an architecture of wood and plaster in which columns, lintels and additional members were designed to support the roof. Two-thirds of the internal space existed for no other reason than to enhance the external appearance of the building, and most of that space was hidden from view by a false ceiling. Since the walls were non-supporting, the columns took the weight of the heavy tile roof and the great quantities of woodwork employed to give it greater height. In order to do this, a series of evenly spaced supporting points were provided in the form of brackets that rose above the columns and were coupled with others that projected forward from the wall plane. While thoroughly functional, the bracketing system has always been regarded as of great aesthetic importance to a building. For centuries it served as virtually the only external 'decoration'; plastered areas were painted white and the woodwork red.

The first structural systems came from Korea, the later ones directly from China. The Japanese made minor variations of these and combined details of more than one, but it is probably true to say that they never actually invented a system of their own. Such systems produced regularly repeated units of space and linear surfaces, and the structural parts that continued through the wall plane related organically the exterior and interior of a building.

A hipped roof style was the usual Chinese preference for centrally-placed halls. The Japanese preferred a combination of a hipped and gable roof, adequately described as hipped-gable. Seen from the front, the lines dropped vertically at either end of the main ridge, then flared at a flattened angle to the four corners. Most roofs of early temple buildings have been reconstructed in later times with structural modifications and greater height. The tiles themselves were laid on boards over rafters.

The building was raised on a platform of tamped earth whose four sides were surfaced in stone. Ordinarily, several stone steps were centred on the north and south sides, and sometimes on the east and west. The size of the platform was exceeded slightly by the reach of the eaves, guiding the rainwater beyond the platform where it dropped into a

Fig. 24

Plate 42

Plates 48, 50

Plate 26

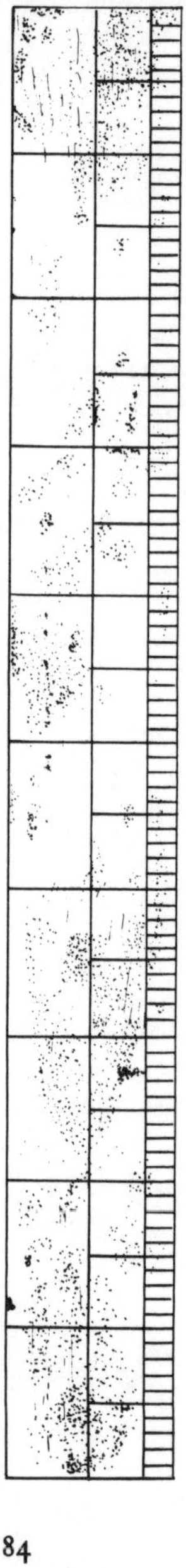

stone-paved gutter or, in the case of less sophisticated buildings, into a surrounding belt of pebbles. Where little is left of a building today, digging frequently exposes the remains of this rainwater trough.

Buildings were easily dismantled for major repairs or the replacement of important parts. This was necessary sometimes for the centre pole of a pagoda, and many buildings are known to have been moved and re-erected in other places. *Hinoki*, Japanese cypress, red pine and varieties of cedar (*sugi*), oak and fir were the chief woods used.

The earliest temples in Japan were built with the Koma *shaku* or Korean foot as the unit of measurement. It was then a fraction larger than the historic Japanese shaku which is 1.158 of the English foot. It apparently came in from north Korea when the Asuka-dera was started in 588 and remained in use for the temples that were built on the Paekche (Kudara) longitudinal plan. The Kawahara-dera (660's) was based on a composite unit, and the Yakushi-ji (around 690) on the Kara shaku, the Chinese foot that became the Nara shaku in Japan.

After the receipt of the first statue from Paekche, when Soga Iname no Sukune made the effort to test the effectiveness of the Buddhist para-phernalia, he 'purified his house at Mukuhara and made it a temple', according to the Nihon Shoki.[4] The 'temple' was burnt by opposition families after a plague struck and the statue was thrown into the Naniwa canal. The Nihon Shoki also supplies the information that a stone statue of Miroku brought from Paekche was put in a temple building in 584 during the reign of Bidatsu, and a pagoda was erected by Umako no Sukune in the following year. This is the first reference to a pagoda. It is said that Emperor Bidatsu gave up his Buddhist ways, following which various calamities befell the country, not the least of which was a plague of smallpox that killed him and many of his people. One of the Mono-nobe burned down the pagoda and then the temple. The remains of the image went into the disposal system of Buddhist ritual equipment, the Naniwa canal.

Fig. 25 Ivory foot (shaku) rule marked with units of Sun and bu, kept in Shōsōin, Nara city. Length 29.6 cm.; width 3.53 cm.; thickness 1 cm. Eighth century

These events brought on some reflection on miracles and the cause for 'punishment', and with the accession of Yōmei, who had been brought up in a Buddhist-oriented family, the temple was rebuilt. The significance of these events is simply that the tide had turned. Disasters came to be regarded as the result of failure to worship the Buddha rather than reprisals by the local *kami*. The date of 585 marked the turning point in this type of thinking, after which the aristocracy were free to construct temples if they so desired.

Several early temples are referred to in the old literature for which little other information is available.[5] The first reference to monumental sculpture is at the time of Yōmei's death in 587 when the son of Shiba Tattō volunteered to carve a *jōroku* statue, that is a 16 ft (*i.e.* large) statue, and build a temple. This was the temple at Sakata,[6] a temple otherwise said to have been built by Tori in 608, also called Kongō-ji, in Takechi village, Nara prefecture.

Wealthy families built and maintained temples as did the emperor and members of his family. Temples as institutions were inclined to accumulate wealth, and monks themselves found ways of increasing their own incomes. During the eighth century the power of the temples reached its peak and was regarded by Emperor Kammu as detrimental to the management of the government, a situation that led him to move the capital and leave the temples behind. Imperially supported temples fared in proportion to imperial fortunes. The crown's eighth century Provincial Temples were all too vivid an illustration of the consequences of the deterioration of imperial power when it appeared as though the support should devolve on the local populace. Not only were they not rebuilt when destroyed in later centuries but some of the destruction itself seems to have been the work of arsonists.

The excavation of temple sites has kept up with all other rapidly developing fields in Japanese archaeology since the second World War. It started with work on the Hōryū-ji in 1939 when the temple came in for fundamental repairs. Since that time vast improvements have been made in techniques and almost every major temple and numerous minor ones have been excavated. Most informative have been the excavations at temples which are fairly well known through the old literature but where almost nothing but nondescript buildings stand on the spot today. Notable among these would be the Asuka-dera and Kawahara-dera.

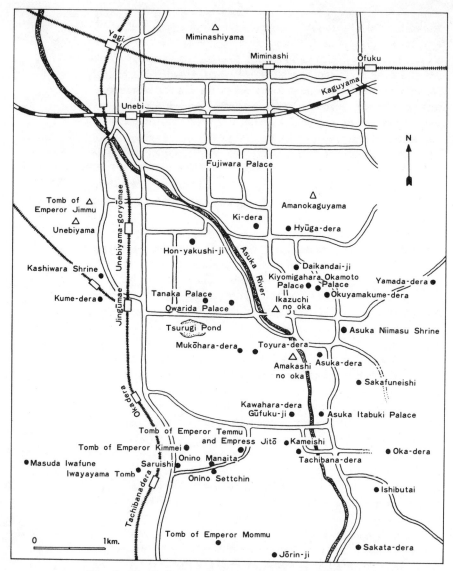

Fig. 26　The Asuka region, Takechi county, Nara prefecture

The date of 588 is customarily accepted for the founding of the Asuka-dera through the reference to the arrival of two temple carpenters, a bronze caster, four tile makers and one painter from Paekche. Wood was cut in the hills in 590. In the 10th month of 592 the Main Hall and cloister of the temple were erected. On the 15th day of the 1st month of 593 the relics were placed in the base stone of the pagoda and on the following day the centre pole was put up. The temple was finished three years later.

The Asuka-dera was excavated in 1956–57. What was revealed at that time has forced a radical revision of the theories regarding the beginnings of Buddhist architecture in Japan. The temple is frequently mentioned in the ancient literature, where it is spoken of as the Hōkō-ji and later in Nara, the Gankō-ji. It played the historic role as temple of the capital; Soga no Umako was its founder and it must have been Umako who invited the craftsmen from Paekche. Two Korean monks took up quarters in the temple in 593. A bronze image ordered by Empress Suiko was cast in 606 by Kuratsukuri no Tori.

Plate 52

Relatively little is heard of the temple after the capital was moved from Asuka, but a fire in 1196 destroyed the pagoda and the Middle Main Hall. These were never rebuilt, and other buildings and the cloister slowly but surely disappeared. Today it is a small temple called the Ango-in, and houses a large disfigured Shaka statue, presumably the original one made by Tori but badly damaged and quite reshaped by later repairs.

The plan had always been assumed to be in the so-called Kudara Style. The excavations proved otherwise. The cloister was latitudinal in orientation and enclosed four buildings, the central one of which was a pagoda. The others were three halls, called Main Halls by most scholars, of roughly equal size, one behind the pagoda and two facing it on either side. A Lecture Hall of exceptional size stood north of the cloister; its fine base stones with column holes and two steps were exposed. It is thought that the bell-tower and sūtra repository lay outside the cloister. All of the buildings were aligned with true north.

Fig. 27

The only comparable plan is a large temple near Pyongyang in north Korea, in which an octagonal building formed the centre unit. It is the Chongam-ni (Japanese: Seigan-ri), known only by its foundations

Fig. 28

87

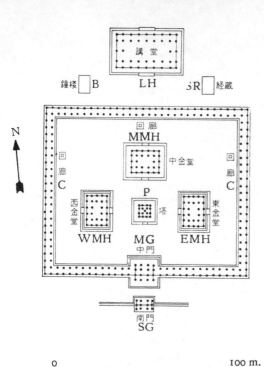

講堂

鐘楼 B　　　LH　　　SR 経蔵

N

回廊
MMH

回廊　中金堂　回廊
C　　　　　　　　　C

西金堂　　P　　東金堂
WMH　MG　EMH
中門

南門
SG

0　　　　　　　　　　100 m.

Fig. 27　Plan of Asuka-dera, in Asuka village, Takechi county, Nara prefecture. 588

Fig. 28　Plan of Chongam-ni, a large destroyed temple near Pyong-yang, north Korea, the probable model for the Asuka-dera

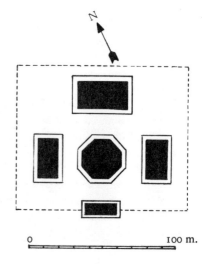

N

0　　　　　　　　　　100 m.

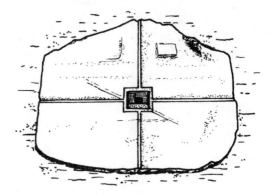

Fig. 29   Top of base stone for centre pole of pagoda, with square hole and relic repository, Asuka-dera. Width c. 200 cm

today. The ten-petalled lotus flower, circular roof tiles, however, are more comparable to examples from Paekche than north Korea.

The Asuka-dera had an unusual approach composed of a paved road 29 m. in length and 2 m. wide leading to the South Gate. Just inside the gate was another paved area. It is recorded that the emperor paid many visits to the temple; perhaps the approach had been uniquely groomed especially for these imperial visits.

In the layout of the temple, the pagoda was situated forward of the juncture of the diagonal lines connecting the corners of the cloister, and the north walls of the two side halls lay along the east-west median line. This left a spacious courtyard area behind the main buildings. All the garan buildings were centred on the pagoda, which stood on a square platform 12 by 12 m. An immense granite stone 2 m. across, buried 2.5 m. below the surface of the earth platform, acted as the support for the centre pole, with a squarish hole for the column 30 by 31 cm. wide, and 21 cm. deep. Furrows on the top of the stone were intended to carry water away from the foot of the column and from the relics buried beneath it. Cut into the east wall of the bottom of the hole is a cavity for relics which is a precise 12 cm. cube. The interior of this little cavity was painted red throughout; it was probably once covered by a stone since a painted stone was found somewhat above it.

After the pagoda had been destroyed by lightning and fire, monks dug under the remains of the pole and rescued a number of objects. These were reburied about 60 cm. below the surface in a wooden box encased between depressions in a pair of stones, and included about

Plate 53

Fig. 29

89

Fig. 30 Examples of glass and jade beads and gold sheet among the relics of the Asuka-dera. Length of lower left object 6.4 cm. Sixth century

Fig. 30

2,500 glass beads and other small objects, as well as an inscribed bell-shaped gilt bronze reliquary of the Kamakura period. The inscription offers the information that the things were removed after the fire and soon replaced. Apparently the twelfth century monks gave up too soon. Lying deeper, on top of the base stone, were glass beads, gold rings, horse bells, small gilt bronze repoussé ornaments, gold sheet, tubular and curved jade beads and, to one side, a suit of armour. All of these objects are indistinguishable from grave-goods in late mounded tombs; in other words, the relics are of a very early date, at a time when there was nothing in the way of religious paraphernalia to draw on for such purposes.

SHITENNŌ-JI

Tradition accepts the year of 593 as the start of the Shitennō-ji on the basis of a Nihon Shoki entry, but there is no month or day included, suggesting that most of the documentation on its beginning was lost before the eighth century. This temple is looked upon as the next style to appear, and the early date is confirmed by the roof tiles and the deep-set stone for the centre pole located 3.5 m. below the platform of the pagoda.

The Shitennō-ji, in the Tennōji part of Osaka city, was erected by Prince Shōtoku to honour the Four Heavenly Kings and remains today a specially hallowed spot for the prince's relics. Its importance also lies in the fact that it is the sole survivor of the Kudara Style of temple. Among the many ravages it has suffered was a serious typhoon in 1934 and aerial bombing in 1945. It is known to have been rebuilt several times and its latest reconstruction is in ferro-concrete, reproducing all the details normally seen in wood.

Plate 22

The excavations that started in 1955 and went hand in hand with the reconstruction of the temple disclosed several startling facts. The Lecture Hall was unusually shallow; its platform measured 33 by 15 m. Collapsed rafters, buried in the ground, with a 'wind bell' and rafter-end bronze ornament, had been painted with red lead. There was a single layer of radially-projecting round rafters to an eave, along with a 'tail' rafter. No extant early buildings have this radial system, although a radial system was later introduced in the Kamakura period. The details of this later system, however, do not correspond with what was found here, but since radial rafters are known to have been in common use on the continent[7] at a suitably early date, their appearance here should not be totally unexpected. The brackets on the Tamamushi Shrine do not project at right angles, but that fact may have nothing to do with the rafters of the Shitennō-ji.

Fig. 31

The Main Hall was almost square, like most early Japanese examples; its platform measured 18.4 by 15.5 m. The structures tended to be placed forward in the courtyard and spacious views were provided of the Lecture Hall which by its very shape had taken on the characteristics of a façade. However, the colonnading of the cloister was poorly co-ordinated with the columns of both the Lecture Hall and the Middle Gate.

Fig. 32

Fig. 23

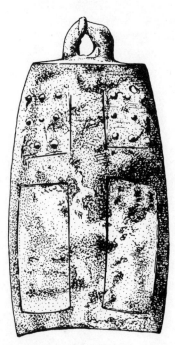

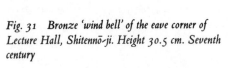

Fig. 31   Bronze 'wind bell' of the eave corner of Lecture Hall, Shitennō-ji. Height 30.5 cm. Seventh century

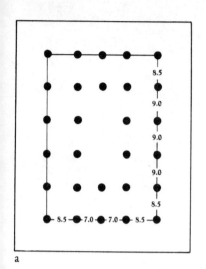

a

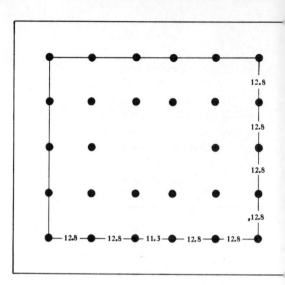

Fig. 32 Plans of Asuka and Hakuhō period buildings showing intercolumniation:
(a) East Main Hall, Asuka-dera; 588; (b) Main Hall, Shitennō-ji; 593; (c)
Middle Main Hall, Kawahara-dera; after 660; (d) Main Hall, Hōryū-ji; after 670

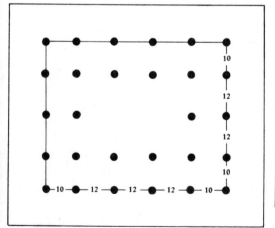

c

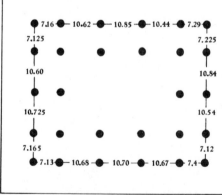

The next temple of real note to go up, but whose documentation is also not without question, was the Ikaruga/dera (also called Wakakusa/dera) or the first Hōryū/ji. According to an inscription on the back of the halo of a bronze sculpture of Yakushi, this temple was built by Prince Shōtoku in 607. Many temples have been traditionally associated with the prince; most of these relationships were undoubtedly greatly exag/ gerated and some were clearly fabricated; nevertheless, Buddhism in Japan owed him a great debt for, if nothing else, he transformed the Soga's magical religion to a devotional one. The religion was largely non/sectarian at the time, although images were made of Shaka, Yakushi and Miroku. Four of the so/called Six Nara Sects were actually known in Japan in the seventh century (Jōjitsu and Sanron, 625; Hossō, 654; and Kusha, 658), but hardly yet formalized. The other two, Kegon and Ritsu, were introduced *c*. 736 and 753 respectively.

Prince Shōtoku is more directly connected with seven temples. Even these seven vary from list to list, but when the selection of a site seems to have been solely his in virgin territory, as the Hōryū/ji, Shitennō/ji and Kōryū/ji were, the location was almost always a low plateau with a fine southern view, protected by hills in the north, and a ready water supply. As some evidence of both his efforts and the inspiration he was to others, a check of the temples a year after his death in 623 noted the existence of forty/six, housing 816 monks and 569 nuns. Over half of these were probably in Nara prefecture.

The prince erected temples exclusively in the Kudara Plan. His own Ikaruga/dera has recently been re/excavated, leaving no question re/ garding its original layout. It was typical of that time period, with successive buildings lying along a single axis, its orientation aligned twenty degrees to the west of north.

Fig. 33

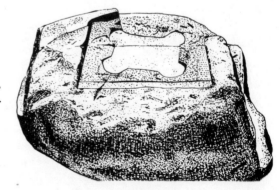

Fig. 33   Base stone for centre pole of pagoda, Ikaruga/dera (or Wakakusa/dera), in the grounds of Hōryū/ji. Length 2.95 m. Probably 607

KAWAHARA-DERA

Fig. 41

Plate 23

Archaeology has proved the next stage in temple planning to be represented by the Kawahara-dera, lying across the fields and the river from the Asuka-dera and below Shōtoku's Tachibana-dera. Documents are missing which detail its beginnings, but it appears in the old literature after 660 and its tiles certainly belong to the latter half of the seventh century. Fortunately, a good deal of archaeological work was possible in the neighbouring fields of the present small temple which is now the home of some of the early statues, and a full complement of buildings was recorded before most of the land was returned to cultivation.

Fig. 34   Plans of (left) Kawahara-dera, in Asuka village, Takechi county, Nara prefecture; after 660; and (right) Kanzeon-ji, at Dazaifu, Dazaifu-chō, Tsukushi county, Fukuoka; seventh century

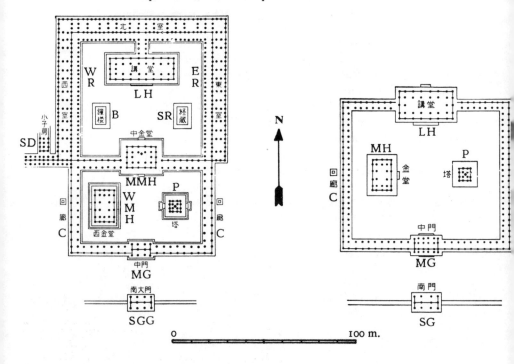

94

The courtyard was small, only about half the size of that at the Asuka-dera, and into this was squeezed a pagoda on the east and a Main Hall facing it on the west. A five by four bay Middle Main Hall stood in the north, pushed back so that its south wall lay on a line with the cloister. The locations of the belfry and sūtra repository were not found, but it has been generally accepted that they were simple buildings within the courtyard. The nine by four bay Lecture Hall was the largest in all early temples. The spot has been partially disturbed by a residence, but the platform size was shown to be about 40 by 16 m. Around the outer edges of the cloister on three sides were forty-three cells, occupying two or three bays at a time. Except for the corners, the sequence was standard-ized: 3:2:2:3:2:2:3, etc.

Fig. 34

The pagoda was rebuilt once during the Middle Ages after a fire. The top of the platform has been scraped off, but calculations showed that the central base stone was at least 1.1 m. below the surface. The stone is about 2 m. in width and has a receptacle hole for the column 1 m. in diameter and 6 cm. deep.

The five by four bay West Main Hall had long eaves and an inter-columniation sequence on the east and west sides of 10:12:12:12:10 in foot units. Since the standard Asuka intercolumniation is almost equal and this sequence is close to the Main Hall of the Yakushi-ji toward the end of the century, it has been speculated that the 'proto-Nara' style of structure and bracketing was coming in at the Kawahara-dera.[8] The decorative double-petal lotus on the end tiles corresponds favourably with other known examples of the second half of the seventh century.

Fig. 35

Fig. 41

The Sūfuku-ji in Shiga prefecture, erected by Emperor Tenchi, is smaller but rather similar in plan to the Kawahara-dera. The steep hillside terrain complicated the planning, and makes the layout difficult to understand today; the stone bases of the wooden columns are all that remain. Both the Koma-dera in Kyoto prefecture and the Minami-shiga-hai-ji in Shiga prefecture have Main Halls so small that they resemble pagodas in their ground plans. They have even been mistaken for double pagoda temples that began to appear near the end of the century. Conceivably, the Main Halls were reduced in size to achieve a balance between two disparate buildings.

Fig. 36

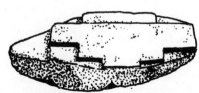

Fig. 35 Striped granite stone base for column of West Main Hall, Kawahara-dera. Length 160 cm.

HŌRYŪ-JI

No documents are more confusing than those dealing with the destruction of Prince Shōtoku's Ikaruga-dera and nothing is more frustrating
than the lack of documents on its rebuilding. Doubts have even been
cast on seemingly acceptable inscriptions on the back of the aureoles of
Plates 30, 31   the bronze figure of Yakushi, supposedly dated 607, and the Shaka triad,
made in 623 by Tori, the year after the prince's death.⁹ Among the many
conflicting reports on the fire, the most satisfactory are the two dates in
the Nihon Shoki, one for 669, the other for 670. They are probably drawn
from two traditions, but that is immaterial. The latter reference is more
informative: fire so destroyed the temple that not a building was left.¹⁰
Later records on the rebuilding may have been lost. Some scholars
theorize, for instance, that the well known *Hōryū-ji-engi-shizai-chō*, a
detailed inventory compiled in 747, is incomplete because of the
omission of all references to such important parts of the temple as the
Lecture Hall and the wall paintings in the Main Hall.

Fig. 38   The Hōryū-ji is composed of two main parts: the Sai-in, the west
sub-temple, and the Tō-in, the east sub-temple. The former is the
replacement temple built after 670, but is situated north and west of
the ruined Ikaruga-dera which remained as a largely unused spot. The
Sai-in was the culmination of decades of juggling a pagoda and a Main
Hall within the garan, arriving at this point with the Main Hall turned
to face the south. The latter, the Tō-in, is an eighth century memorial to
the prince, on the spot occupied by the Ikaruga Palace.

The paradox of this scheme at the Sai-in is that it appears to be
combined with older individual features in the architecture that are
usually regarded as characteristic of the Asuka period, in contrast to a
traditional Hakuhō date: cloud brackets, inverted V-shaped brackets,
an additional square plate at the top of each column, rough stone bases,
entasis, and reduction in size in upper levels of buildings. Apparently
many of the stone bases were brought over from the Ikaruga-dera and
used for the Hōryū-ji buildings, but the intercolumniation should have
been adjusted to the incoming structural style. In fact, the intercolumni-
Fig. 32   ation of the Main Hall was again close to the Yakushi-ji, and helps to
date the building late in the century.

It is now recognized that the Japanese did not simply follow basic
imported plans with a minimum of modification. They tried several

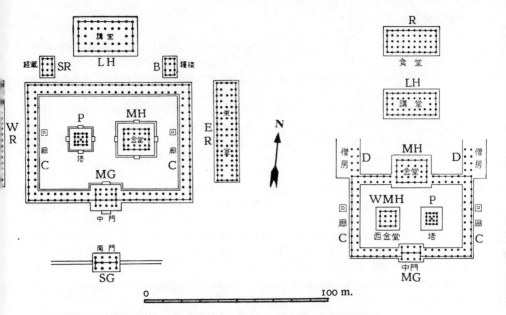

R
食堂

LH
講堂

講堂
LH

経蔵 SR   B 鐘楼

W
R

P
塔

MH
金堂

E
R
東室

MG
中門

N

僧房 D

MH
金堂

D 僧房

回廊 C

WMH
西金堂

P
塔

回廊 C

中門
MG

南門
SG

0   100 m.

Fig. 36   Plans of (left) Sai-in of Hōryū-ji, Ikaruga-machi, Ikoma county, Nara prefecture; after 670; and (right) Minami-shiga-hai-ji, in Ōtsu city, Shiga prefecture; late seventh century

Fig. 37   Bronze ornament for the end of a rafter of the pagoda, Hōryū-ji. Height 13 cm. Late seventh century

approaches, but it was always nothing more than rarified romanticism to credit the plan of the Hōryū-ji to the Japanese aesthetic sense of Prince Shōtoku and the two openings of the Middle Gate to his interests in social equality, as was occasionally done by some writers who dis-counted the fire. The prince had been dead almost half a century when the Hōryū-ji was rebuilt. In fact, a full view of the interior of the garan

Fig. 36

from the Middle Gate could hardly be called 'Japanese' at all. It lacks the piecemeal revelation and the elements of mystery so highly praised by at least later aestheticians. But the compensations in reaching a balance border on genius. The cloister is one bay longer on the east side and so provides more room around the Main Hall; the pagoda is roughly twice the height of the Main Hall and both occupy approximately the same amount of cubic space and are thus weighed against each other,[11]

Fig. 37
Plate 32

the lines of the pagoda are progressively flatter in ascending order until the top, at which point the lines are angled sharply, and give the effect of anchoring the building. It may well be that the two openings of the

Plates 24, 25

unique Middle Gate are related to the panoramic concept of the garan, and were to be co-ordinated with the two chief buildings of the courtyard.

The Middle Gate is said by the Japanese to be like a baby on its mother's back. The upper level is a reduced version of the lower one. Only the central columns form continuous vertical lines. Essentially, the lines of the gate follow those of the cloister which set the direction for the entire unit.

A fire on the night of January 26, 1949, destroyed the Main Hall and damaged its famous wall paintings beyond repair. Luckily, as the

Plates 26, 27

building was in the process of restoration, all of its portable religious objects had been removed. Constructed in the same style as the Middle Gate and pagoda, the upper level was strongly recessed and cut to one less bay on each side. The inverted V-shaped bracket was consistently employed and the cloud brackets were outlined in relief carving. Both the Main Hall and pagoda were given the additional porch on the lowest level, apparently added around 711 to protect the recently installed religious furnishings.

The Lecture Hall was destroyed by fire in 925 and replaced by another building brought in before the end of the century. In an effort towards avoiding a recurrence of this disaster, the new Lecture Hall was pushed well back, allowing the bell-tower and sūtra repository to be included

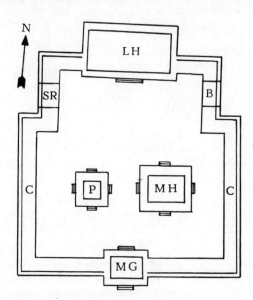

Fig. 38 Plan of Sai-in of Hōryū-ji after the tenth century when the Lecture Hall, Sūtra Repository and Belfry were incorporated into the cloister, the Lecture Hall misaligned

in the changed, angular lines of the cloister and consequently drastically redistributing the space.

There have been endless arguments over whether the original Lecture Hall stood outside the cloister, as at the Asuka-dera, or formed a northern link in the cloister, as at the Shitennō-ji. The medieval text which says the Lecture Hall was located farther back after the fire also says it was built where the Hokushitsu (north hall) had stood. From this one would assume that the old Lecture Hall was situated in front of the present one and occupied the mid-part of the north cloister.

The 1935 excavations yielded no remains of this north hall, and the rainwater trough of the cloister was found to have crossed the back of the garan. The eighth century Hōryū-ji inventory refers to the refectory in dimensions that do not match those of the Lecture Hall, so Asano assumes that the Lecture Hall had not yet been built in 747 when the document was drafted.[12] This is not accepted by all, but it is certainly a plausible interpretation of the excavation results. The present Lecture Hall has apparently been modified somewhat since it was first erected; it is off the main axis of the garan.

The base stone for the pagoda's central column is about 2.6 m. below the surface of the platform. It was discovered in 1926 that the foot of the

Fig. 38

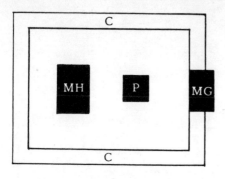

Fig. 39   Original plan of Tachibana-dera, oriented to the east, in Asuka village, Takechi county, Nara prefecture; early seventh century

pole had rotted away, leaving it suspended in place. This called for a reassessment of the theories regarding the centre pole, for under such circumstances, it could hardly be said to be making a major contribution to the structure of the building. It is now recognized that it stands almost independently, supporting the metal ceremonial umbrellas and other ornaments of the spire and, equally important, it symbolizes the cosmic axis. The builders themselves must have expected far less of the centre pole than did later architecture historians.

The balancing of the buildings against each other was in all probability the result of interaction between aesthetic and ritual interests. There was considerable experimenting, and a steady reduction, from three Main Halls at the Asuka-dera, through two at the Kawahara-dera, to one at the Hōryū-ji. Unlike Murata[13] the line seems best drawn to the Hōryū-ji not from the Shitennō-ji but from the Asuka-dera by way of the Tachibana-dera and Kawahara-dera.

Some of the Hōryū-ji's art objects were salvaged from the first temple, if one can believe the dates on the inscriptions. The bronze Yakushi served as the chief icon of the temple into at least the eighth century and perhaps longer, until it was supplanted by the gilt bronze Shaka triad that had been finished in 623 by the court-employed Tori. Tori's family were ardent Buddhists. His grandfather, Shiba Tattō (or Tachitō), had arrived from China in 522; his father was a statue maker and Tori, or Shiba Kuratsukuribe no Obito Tori as he is called in the inscription on the aureole of the Shaka triad, may be credited with the major advances in the art of casting Buddhist figures in the late sixth and early seventh centuries. Old textual references suggest that he was also a painter. The Shaka was made 'life-size', but this is not to suggest that portraiture of any sort was intended, or even possible at that time. The style is rather

Fig. 39

Plate 30

Plate 31

detached and is designed to play down the physical aspects of the figure while enhancing its spiritual qualities. The figure is a transposition into bronze of Chinese Wei dynasty images and consequently softer and more abstract in the sense that the ornamental value of the hair, drapery, lotus and tendril patterns in the halo and aureole are all consciously stressed.

The polychromed Four Heavenly Kings of camphor wood came from this or another earlier temple and are Japan's oldest. Such figures were then regarded as guardians of the realm. The appearance of a sculptor's name in the inscriptions on two of their haloes and in the text of the Nihon Shoki is generally used to date the sculptures to the middle of the seventh century. They are in a stiff, blocky style, emphasizing surface detail. The scarf that hangs down and curves forward on either side is some concession to satisfactory viewpoints for visitors walking round the Buddha platform.

The remnants of an embroidered paradise scene, ordered as a memorial for Shōtoku by his wife soon after his death, now kept in the Chūgū-ji,

Fig. 40   Plan of Main Hall, Hōryū-ji. The large walls, panels 1, 6, 9 and 10, had paintings of Buddha groups, the others, bodhisattvas. Copies of the original paintings are now affixed to the walls

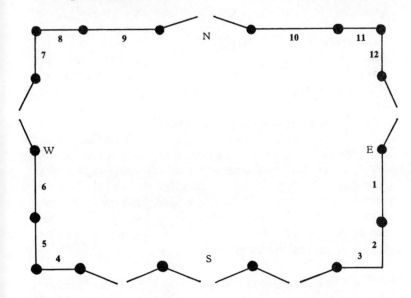

is tantalizing evidence of a remarkable level of textile craftsmanship. Called Tenjūkoku Mandala (Mandala of the Land of Heavenly Longevity), it is now a patchwork of preserved fragments that make no coherent pattern, only about one-sixteenth the original size of the hanging. It may have initially resembled the painted paradises on the walls of the Buddhist caves at Tun-huang in north-west China, and at least helps to explain the depth of tradition in Japan which led to the painted paradises in the Hōryū-ji's Main Hall.

The wall paintings are not mentioned in the 747 inventory, and it is occasionally argued that they had not yet been done at that time.[14] A pagoda's iconographic scheme included wall paintings and a set of sculptures of Shaka, Amida, Yakushi and Miroku facing the cardinal directions. Nothing was so standardized for Main Halls and few received wall paintings, but these Buddhas became the subjects of the four large wall panels in the Main Hall of the Hōryū-ji and were supplemented with bodhisattvas on the eight small panels.

Identification of the Buddhas and their paradises, assuming that by now Miroku had been elevated to a Buddha, has been made more difficult by fungal and other deterioration which started at an early date, by conflicting statements in several medieval texts, and by the lack of similar, prior material. There is reasonable concensus on the smaller panels which were reproduced almost identically in the pagoda, perhaps about 740, and plastered over later. Running clockwise from the south-east corner they were Nikkō (2), Kannon (3), Seishi (4), Gakkō (5), Kannon (7), Monju (8), Fugen (11) and an eleven-headed Kannon (12). Mizuno has made the most satisfactory identification of the large Buddhas, the first two of which have been recognized for some time: east wall (1), Shaka; west wall (6), Amida; north-west wall (9), Yakushi; and north-east wall (10), Miroku.[15]

In stylistic terms, the full body form, thin, almost transparent drapery and a special kind of shading, may be traced at least to Central Asia; the grouping of the figures would appear to be more Chinese; the colour balances and details of rhythm and adaptation in the small panels—for example, the standing bodhisattvas are under beads while the seated bodhisattvas are under canopies—may perhaps be more locally Japanese, but the features as a whole represent the pervasively internationalized style of the early eighth century.

Fig. 40

Fig. 41   Type examples of round eave-end tiles and pantiles; (a) Wakakusa-dera;
diameter of round tile 15 cm.; 607; (b) Kawahara-dera; diameter 18.6 cm.; after
660; (c) Hōryū-ji; diameter 18.6 cm.; after 670; (d) Oka-dera; diameter 18.3 cm.;
second half of seventh century; (e) Tōshōdai-ji; diameter 15.3 cm.; c. 760

HŌRIN-JI AND HOKKI-JI

Two small temples lie to the north-east of the Hōryū-ji and are separated by ten minute walks across the fields. On the west is the Hōrin-ji and on the east the Hokki-ji. The former is supposed to have been built in 622 by Yamashiro no Ōe, the eldest son of Prince Shōtoku, as a place to pray for his father's recovery from an illness, and the latter in 638 by priest Fukuryō, to fulfill the prince's last wishes. The plan of the Hōrin-ji is identical to that of the Hōryū-ji, only much smaller, so it may be assumed that in 622 it was just a small prayer chapel around which the temple was later elaborated, using the Hōryū-ji as its model. It has no old buildings today; the last of these was the small three-storey pagoda that was destroyed by fire in 1944.

The other temple is about the same size and was also probably at first only an insignificant chapel. It stands on the spot where the prince had his Okamoto Palace and, as a result, it sometimes goes by the name of Okamoto-dera. It is said that the prince requested that his palace be converted into a temple, a practice that gained great popularity in later centuries. A circular metal member at the foot of the spire carried an inscription (recorded only in an old document): 'This pagoda (was) the desire of priest Keisei in Temmu 14 and was completed in Keiun 3.' These dates are 685 and 706.

Fig. 42

Excavated in 1960, the Hokki-ji's basic plan was confirmed to be the reverse of the Hōryū-ji plan; in other words, the pagoda was on the east side, the Main Hall on the west. This plan is called the Hokki-ji Style.[16] A wall surrounded the garan whose buildings were both closely-spaced and unusually large for their setting, leaving little freedom of movement for visitors. The three-storey pagoda was well harmonized with the low rectangular buildings. Its architectural details are close to those of the Hōryū-ji, but the overhang of the eaves is proportionally much greater than usual. Since the storeys show an extraordinary degree of similarity to the first, third and fifth storeys of the pagoda of the Hōryū-ji, it might be theorized that the latter, less its alternate storeys, served as the model without other reduction in size.

Plates 33, 34

Monks of the Ikaruga-dera constructed three temples after the 670 fire while trying to decide where to rebuild, according to the records. These were the Hachioka-dera (or Kōryū-ji in Kyoto), Takai-dera and Hōrin-ji (also called Mii-dera). If this is the case, there would have been

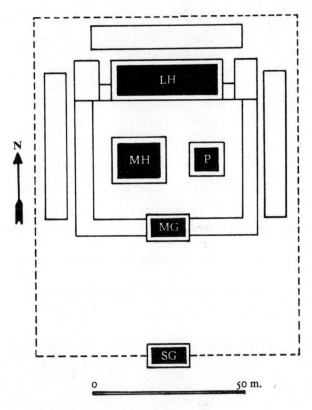

Fig. 42   Plan of Hokki-ji, in Ikaruga-machi, Ikoma county, Nara prefecture. c. 685

next to nothing standing on the Hōrin-ji spot when the Ikaruga-dera was destroyed. As for the Kōryū-ji, there is a document giving a date of 603 for the donation of a statue of Miroku by Prince Shōtoku to Hata Kawakatsu, who then built a temple, so that a similar situation must have prevailed at that spot, if the monks 'built' a temple where one was already supposed to exist. One assumes, in other words, that these were initially small chapels which were later converted into full temples.

The fact that the Hokki-ji and Hōrin-ji are variations of the panoramic plan shows that no absolute conditions governed the arrangement. On the basis of excavations and the few extant examples of these early temples, the development in types and geographic spread is seen in this chart, based on research by Ishida, in which all the variations are included:[17]

Plan	Number of temples	In Kinki	In Outer Provinces	Number with Asuka period tiles
Kudara (Shitennō-ji)	11	9	2	9
Hōryū-ji	16	12	4	11
Hokki-ji	16	8	8	8

As time passed a proportionally larger number of temples were built in the provinces; these tended to have later roof tiles and the Hokki-ji Style was favoured while this trend was taking place. It should be remembered that all of these temples were single pagoda types and that the Shitennō-ji plan was characteristic of the Middle Asuka I (late Asuka) period, whereas the Hōryū-ji and Hokki-ji plans were essentially characteristic of the Middle Asuka II (early Hakuhō) period.

YAKUSHI-JI

In the year 680, according to the Nihon Shoki, when Temmu's consort, later Empress Jitō, contracted an eye disease, the emperor ordered the construction of a temple to Yakushi, the Buddha of healing. Yet when the emperor himself became ill six years later and numerous rites and prayers were conducted in several specified temples, the Yakushi-ji is not mentioned, although in 688, which was Jitō's second year, a public ceremony was held there, indicating that the temple was definitely underway. Whatever caused the delay, and it was considerable, not until 697 do the records speak of a ceremony to celebrate the impending completion of the statues. A funeral service was held jointly in the Daian-ji, Yakushi-ji, Gankō-ji (old Asuka-dera) and Gūfuku-ji (Kawahara-dera), according to the Shoku Nihongi, in 703, and it is recognized that by the end of the century the Yakushi-ji had become one of the 'big three' of Fujiwara temples, ranking in importance with the court-supported Daian-ji and Asuka-dera.

After the capital was moved to Heijō, the court's temples inevitably went along, but in this move only the Yakushi-ji kept its plan intact.

Oddly enough, the Shoku Nihongi mentions the transfer of only one of the temples, the Gankō-ji in 716; another version refers to the transfer of the Hōkō-ji (the same temple) in 718, as though the ancient writers also had difficulty with so many names for one temple. But the Yakushi-ji's own *Yakushi-ji-engi*, a document of the Chōwa era (1012–17), gives the same year for its removal, probably using information that had already gone into the Shoku Nihongi.

There is, to amplify, the present temple at Nishinokyō in the old city of Heijō, the site in the Fujiwara area known as Hon-yakushi-ji (Original Yakushi-ji), and a theory that there may have been still one more location of this temple—the place where it was actually started, but whence it was subsequently moved, which might explain the time lost in getting it built. According to this theory, Temmu was constructing two temples symmetrically situated to his Kiyomigahara Palace, the Takechidai-ji (renamed the Daikandai-ji and later the Daian-ji), and the Yakushi-ji, separated by three chō (roughly 360 yards). The Yakushi-ji would then have been on a spot that would have been east of the Fujiwara capital and it would have fallen to the lot of Empress Jitō to move the temple to the Hon-yakushi-ji site. She is known to have followed Temmu's wishes in other ways, but the only evidence at the spot consists of Late Asuka period tiles dredged up from a pond.[18] It has yet to be proved that buildings actually stood there.

The Hon-yakushi-ji made architectural history by being the first temple in Japan with a pair of pagodas. The stone bases for the pagodas and Main Hall are mostly well preserved; the remains of the Lecture Hall and other buildings were either destroyed or lie under an east-west road and modern houses. The transfer to Heijō need not have taken long. Uneven places in the terrain may have required levelling at the new site,[19] and one minor and perhaps insignificant difference involved exchanging the relics from below the east pagoda of the earlier temple to below the west pagoda of the later temple. The hole was covered with a circular stone. The arbitrariness defies explanation, but it is apparent that only one pagoda was religiously functional at the time.

As the first temple to be built with a pair of pagodas, the Yakushi-ji re-introduced the continental preference for symmetry. The east pagoda is the only building of the late Hakuhō style still standing today. Records tell of several fires, but through the diary of the twelfth century pilgrim

Fig. 43
Plates 38, 39

Plates 39, 40

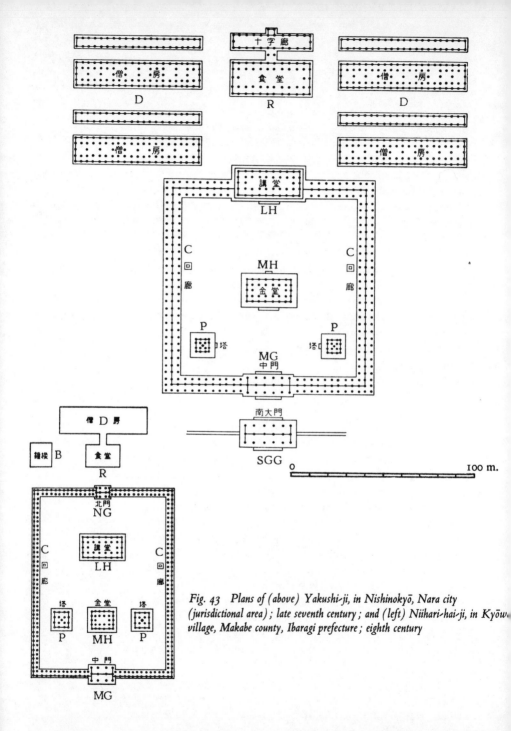

十字廊

食堂

僧　房　　D

僧　房　　D

僧　房

R

講堂
LH

C　　　　　　　　　C
回　　　　　　　　　回
廊　　　　　　　　　廊

MH
金堂

P　　　　　　　　　P
塔　　　　　　　　　塔

MG
中門

僧　D　房

南大門

鐘樓　B　　食堂
　　　　　R

SGG

0　　　　　　　　　　100 m.

北門
NG

講堂
LH

C　　　　　C
回　　　　　回
廊　　　　　廊

塔　　金堂　　塔
P　　MH　　P

中門
MG

Fig. 43   Plans of (above) Yakushi-ji, in Nishinokyō, Nara city
(jurisdictional area); late seventh century; and (left) Niihari-hai-ji, in Kyōw
village, Makabe county, Ibaragi prefecture; eighth century

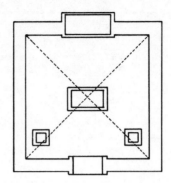

Fig. 44   Planning system of garan of
Yakushi-ji

Ōe no Chikamichi, who visited the great temples of Nara, one knows that the major buildings had lower and upper level 'porches' (*mokoshi*) and were largely intact and in their original form at that time. The west pagoda burned in 1528, was evidently rebuilt, then burned again in 1597 and was never replaced,[20] but by this time as many as four different fires had also destroyed the cloisters, Main Hall and Lecture Hall at least once in each case. The present Main Hall was erected in 1600, directly on the old base stones.

The buildings of the Yakushi-ji compared quite favourably in size with those of the Hōryū-ji, but the garan occupied about twice as much space. The pagodas had the height of five-storied structures, but to utilize the porches, only three stories were possible. The pagodas were pulled out to the corners, affording a roomy forecourt and giving supreme prominence to the Main Hall, now exactly in the centre. There was really no satisfactory single place inside the cloister from which both pagodas could be adequately seen, while from the outside, the cloister hid at least their lower third from view.

Fig. 44

The pagoda is in the 'proto-Nara' structural system. The brackets were duplicated both up and out, and the lever running parallel with the roof was closely cropped, the bracket located at its very end. The rafters directly under each roof were also doubled, the upper level square in section, the lower level round. The duplication of members allows each to be proportionally smaller and to do less work, adding a degree of elegance over the heaviness of the Hōryū-ji -Hokki-ji style.

The porches had no structural value. They did, however, provide a sort of decorative unity to the complex of buildings. There are now no

Figs 45, 46   base stones for these porches at the old Hon-yakushi-ji site, but since the style is inconceivable without them, it may be taken for granted that the stones were small enough to have been carried off easily. These porches look like afterthoughts on the Hōryū-ji's pagoda and Main Hall, but were an integral part of the architecture at the Yakushi-ji. Recent archaeological work shows minor discrepancies in the plan. The South Great Gate stood about one foot east of centre of the north-south axis, and the present South Gate is about two feet west of centre.[21]

Fig. 48   The faithful reproduction of this temple at Heijō attests to its acceptance aesthetically and religiously, yet within the short span of time between its construction at Fujiwara and transfer to Heijō, new stylistic features had overtaken it. The latest advances in Heijō were to be seen in the Daian-ji, whose two pagodas were pulled still farther forward and probably given their own cloisters. In effect they were moved out of the way and set apart from the nucleus of the temple as though dispossessed of religious meaning.

Fig. 43   Other examples of the basic Yakushi-ji plan are the Niihari-hai-ji in Ibaragi prefecture, excavated as far back as 1939, the Kudara-hai-ji in Hirakata city, Osaka prefecture, and the Hiso-dera in Ōyodo-machi, Yoshino county, Nara prefecture, which had tiles of the late seventh century.

The recently arrived continental style emerged in all of the arts: the monumental sculptures of the Yakushi-ji were synchronized with the Main Hall in scale and symmetry. Other temples had their large sculp-

Plates 45, 46   tures, but only here can this development be fully appreciated today.

The bronze seated Yakushi is flanked by a standing Nikkō and Gakkō, the bodhisattvas of the Sun and Moon, all arrayed on a Chinese marble platform. Each holds up the inside hand and together they create

Plate 44   a formal balance that complements the scheme of the architecture. All the figures have the full forms of the early T'ang dynasty style, but not yet the round faces of the Hōryū-ji wall paintings. The supple body curves are heightened by the rather lightly hanging drapery. Both bodhisattvas have holes in the wrists which once held freely draped scarves; these gave even greater three-dimensionality to the figures.

The arguments have been endless as to whether these bronze images were made for the earlier temple or the present one.[22] There has never been any doubt that workshops could produce large bronze sculptures

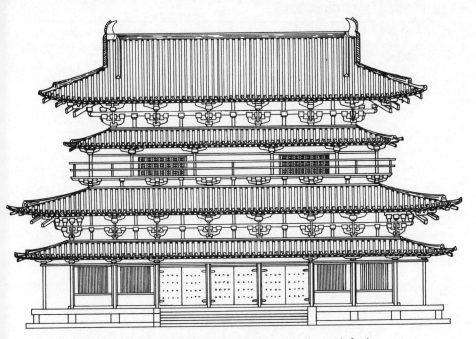

Fig. 45 Modified reconstruction of Main Hall, Yakushi-ji, by author, with five bays on upper level, three doors and four windows on ground level; late seventh century

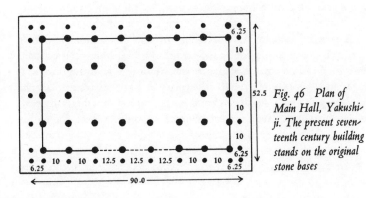

Fig. 46 Plan of Main Hall, Yakushi-ji. The present seventeenth century building stands on the original stone bases

III

Fig. 47 Detail of grape pattern in a narrow frieze along the top of the bronze covering of the socle supporting the Yakushi Buddha, Yakushi-ji, late seventh or early eighth century

at this time; the head from the Yamada-dera, part of a triad made between 678 and 685, is a case in point. The Yakushi-ji problem is compounded by two conflicting texts, one of the eleventh century, the other of the seventeenth. The former says the statues were moved by cart from the old temple in a seven day trip; the latter says the statues were cast at Kanaokiyama by Priest Gyōgi in the Yōrō period (717–724). Kanaokiyama is supposed to be near the present Yakushi-ji, although the priests there today cannot locate it. The date suits the establishment of the temple at Heijō, and Gyōgi was a well known priest who died in 749.

The decoration on the pedestal under Yakushi includes a grape pattern and the Tutelary Deities of the directions, both rarely seen in Japan. Since the latter had been out of style in China for centuries, one is inclined to suggest the earliest possible date for the bronze base if nothing else. Repairs to the Yakushi after the 1952 Yoshino earthquake recovered from under it two Wadō-kaichin coins in mint condition, coins of the seventeenth and eighteenth centuries, a broken gilt bronze statuette of Yakushi and some small gilt bronze ornamental pieces. The presence of the Wadō-kaichin coins was taken to mean that the statue had not been moved since first placed in that position,[23] but this leaves the late coins unexplained.

DAIAN-JI AND GANKŌ-JI

One of the most ambitious projects of early emperors was the Daian-ji; its progress may have been hindered by the sheer magnitude of the undertaking. The 747 archives of the temple say it was located along the Kudara river (probably at Kōryō-chō in Nara prefecture) in Jomei's reign (630's) and supported by 300 households. When it was eventually burnt down, this was interpreted as the wrath of a kami residing in a nearby village. Temmu moved the temple to Yabe village in Takechi county in 673 and named it in the Chinese fashion for official temples, Takechi-daikan-ji (dai-ji = great temple), appointing Priest Dōji as its head and allowing it 200 supporting households. By no later than 682 it was being called Daikandai-ji.[24] Temmu's Kiyomigahara Palace was situated not far away and the temple figured frequently in the activities

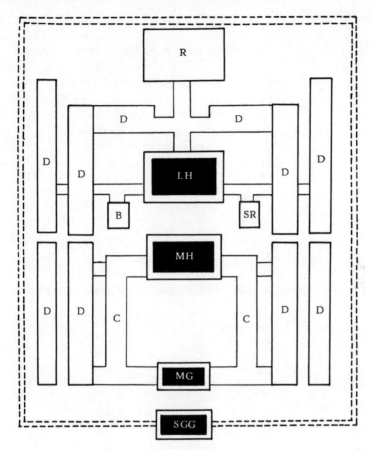

Fig. 48 Plan of Daian-ji, at Daianji-chō, Nara city. After 718

0   100 m.

of the court. Its plan was similar to the Kawahara/dera, but on a much larger scale, and the pagoda was the first to have nine storeys in Japan.

Fig. 48   When the temple was moved to Heijō it received two pagodas and moved ahead of the Yakushi/ji in style. The pagodas were placed well

Fig. 9   ahead of the Middle Gate and probably, as in the largest temples, set off in their own cloisters. This arrangement is called the Daian/ji Style, and was followed at the Tōdai/ji, Saidai/ji, Shin/yakushi/ji, Akishino/dera and Taima/dera, of which only the Taima/dera has two pagodas standing today. The Middle Gate and Main Hall were joined by a cloister and it was not uncommon to have an East Main Hall and a West Main Hall standing outside the garan nucleus.

The Daian/ji rapidly declined when the capital was shifted from Heijō. Buildings quickly disappeared, and even the stone bases for the pagodas were removed around 1889 to be used at the Kashiwara Shrine.²⁵ Excavations in 1954 exposed remains of the South Great Gate, Middle Gate and cloisters. A modest temple is maintained on the spot today, its storehouse preserving the old sculptures.

It was popular to build in a grandiose fashion and the old Asuka/dera was formally moved and re/erected on a large scale in Heijō, renamed the Gankō/ji. It had one cloistered pagoda, placed on the east like the Kōfuku/ji and Tōshōdai/ji, outside the garan cloister. The ground plan

Plate 52   of what was the largest five/storey pagoda built in Japan is perfectly preserved in base stones. Its excavation in 1927 yielded many beads, coins, gold bars and plaques.

HŌRYŪ/JI TŌ/IN

Priest Gyōshin was given the mandate to build a memorial to Prince Shōtoku on the spot where the prince's Ikaruga Palace had stood. Emperor Shōmu's consort made a donation of an imperial residence hall in 739 as a beginning, and this is the building known as the Dempō/dō. The sequence of halls has been modified since the eighth century, when there was a South Gate, Middle Gate, Yumedono, Shichijō/den (named because it was 70 by 20 ft) and Dempō/dō that served as the Lecture Hall. The cloister surrounded the octagonal

Plate 28   Yumedono and was connected to the Middle Gate. Excavations showed that only the roofs of the Yumedono, Dempō/dō and two buildings of the priests' quarters were tiled.²⁶

Fig. 49 Ogre mask corner-ridge tile, Daian-ji. Height 41 cm. Early eighth century

TŌDAI-JI AND KŌFUKU-JI

Emperor Shōmu followed the Chinese practice closely: he ordered the making of a colossal Buddha, and each province was to erect a pagoda and a temple. The Buddha was to be housed in the Tōdai-ji, Shōmu's crowning project, upon which millions of workmen worked for a period of about twenty years.

The first effort to cast the Birushana Buddha was made in a workshop near Shōmu's palace not far from Lake Biwa, but two years of frustration there came to nothing. The workshop was moved to Heijō and a fairly large team of casters headed by a Korean then finished it in approximately four years. Dedication of the Great Buddha took place in 752 in the presence of the abdicated emperor, reigning empress, other members of the royal family and ten thousand guests. The statue itself has suffered so seriously from earthquakes and fires that virtually none of it is original today. The Great Buddha Hall (Daibutsu-den) has been much rebuilt in a Kamakura period structural style, four bays shorter than it was in the eighth century. Its height and depth remain roughly the same.

Fig. 53

115

The fatefully prophetic remark in the temple's records that 'all the copper resources of the country' went into the making of the Great Buddha goes far to explain why there are virtually no bronze statues in succeeding centuries. The temple's own Four Heavenly Kings, which were in bronze according to the archives, are of polychromed, unbaked clay. They stand in the Kaidan‑in. Perhaps even the originals were sacrificed for repairs on the Buddha, its lotus or altar decorations. Many of the sculptures from the affluent years of the Shōmu era stand together in the eastern part of the Sangatsu‑dō on the hillside and constitute the finest single collection of eighth century images in the country.

Fig. 50

Plate 51

An immense wall formed the perimeter of the Tōdai‑ji, with three gates in at least each of the south and west sides. A remaining one on the west is the old Sahōji Gate, now the Tegai Gate. The cloister that defined the garan was colonnaded both inside and out, and the seven‑storey pagodas were about 300 ft high, each set a little back from the centre of its own cloister, which in both cases were poorly aligned with the temple's major axis. Unfortunately, structures with metal masts had no defence against lightning. Soon destroyed by fire, they were never rebuilt.

The 1180 civil war was disastrous for the temple. Some rebuilding took place in 1200, but on a relatively modest scale: the cloister, for instance, was colonnaded only on one side. An earthquake of 1567, which toppled the Buddha's head, left the temple destitute for over a century until the wherewithal could be found for repairs.

The Tōdai‑ji was a far vaster establishment than one imagines today. A manuscript kept in the Shōsōin, whose title may be translated as *Ground Plan of Halls and Houses in Tōdai‑ji*, shows how extensive it really was. Archaeologists used it to identify remains of priests' quarters which were found when a concrete 'Shōsōin' was begun. These quarters were floored with well‑cut tufa blocks and must have required the use of chairs.[27]

Fig. 51

The spacious temple in Nara Park, the Kōfuku‑ji, whose five‑storey pagoda is one of the city's most conspicuous traditional monuments, was moved to Heijō from Yamashina in the Kyoto area as the Fujiwara started their rise to power. It was probably completed in the 730's as the first temple at Heijō to have a set of three Main Halls. The Middle Main Hall was nine by six bays. Space problems resulted in the South Great Gate and Middle Gate being set very close together.

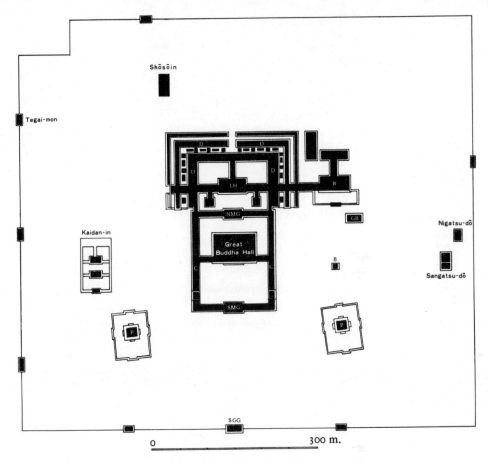

Fig. 50 Plan of Tōdai-ji, in Nara city, as it was built in the eighth century

The identity of the temple with the Fujiwara later made it a prime target. When the Fujiwara backed the wrong family against the Taira, the Kōfuku-ji experienced the same kind of ravaging as its neighbour, the Tōdai-ji. Armed monks temporarily regained some of its prestige and power in the twelfth and thirteenth centuries, but most of its buildings date to even later times.

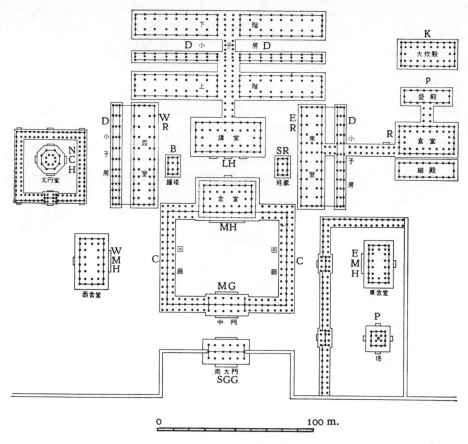

Fig. 51   Plan of Kōfuku-ji, in Tōdaiji-chō, Nara city. Middle of the eighth century

TOSHODAI-JI

A highly valued piece of land, once in the possession of the royal family, was donated to the Chinese priest Chien-chên in appreciation of his response to the invitation to conduct ordination ceremonies at the Tōdai-ji. His efforts to reach Japan had resulted in several shipwrecks, required fourteen years of travel time and cost him his eyesight, but he arrived in 754. Ganjin, as the Japanese called him, had come from the

Lung-hsing-ssŭ in Yang-chou, China, and introduced the Ritsu or
Rules sect to Japan. His Chinese colleagues supervised the making of
the images, as well as the building of the Tōshōdai-ji based on an initial
gift of an Imperial Assembly Hall from the Heijō palace in 759 that
became the Lecture Hall. The east pagoda was donated by an aristocrat
who had served as ambassador to China. No base stones remain today
on its platform.

Plate 47

Plate 48

The massive Main Hall has the classic features of the Nara period:
monumentality, subtle scaling of intercolumniation, a minimum of
entasis and one-third of the wall space devoted to bracketing of the two
up/two out system. The hipped roof has been rebuilt, but its *shibi* (finials
at the ends of the horizontal ridge) are directly above the third and sixth
pillars of the seven by four bay hall, whose centrality is emphasized by
the graded spacing of the columns in feet: 11:13:15:16:15:13:11.
While the progressive narrowing of bays towards the corners is the
natural outcome of the structural system, the fact has been used in its
most effective way in this Main Hall.

Fig. 52
Plates 42, 43

Fig. 53

*Fig. 52   Sections of the structural systems of (left) the 'proto-Nara' style first storey
of pagoda of Yakushi-ji; late seventh century; and (right) Nara style, Main Hall,
Tōshōdai-ji; after 759*

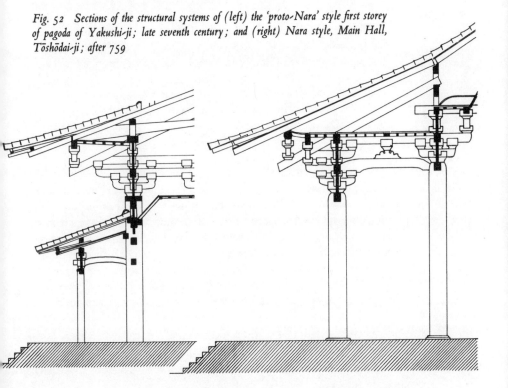

Fig. 53 Plans of
eighth-century buildings in
Nara showing inter-
columniation : (above)
Main Hall, Daian-ji;
(below) Main Hall,
Tōshōdai-ji; and (right)
Great Buddha Hall,
Tōdai-ji

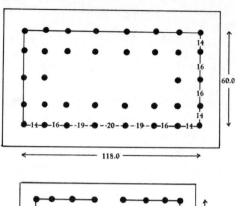

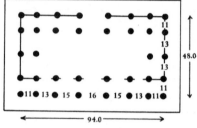

Plate 47

The large dry-lacquer Birushana Buddha was to be seen from outside the building, framed in the doorway, its flanking bodhisattvas visible through the two adjoining bays. In order to arrange this, the entire bay on the south side was left unenclosed, forming a kind of porch. The Main Hall, therefore, represents the ultimate stage in focusing attention on the central Buddha through an ideal co-ordination of images with building. A later narrowing of the doors by strips of wood has changed the effect that had been so meticulously arrived at in the eighth century.

Plate 48

The Lecture Hall is in the process of being entirely overhauled at the time of writing. It has been dismantled, and excavations are going on underneath every square inch of it. This hall had an earthen floor whereas the Main Hall a stone floor. A nine by four bay building, the hipped-gable roof, long and low surface lines and simple bracketing, are all the more characteristically Japanese, and contrast with the more Chinese, volumetric Main Hall.

Ganjin never returned to China. He died in 763 and was entombed in the north-east corner of the compound. The ordination platform, composed of earth brought over from China and later faced with stone,

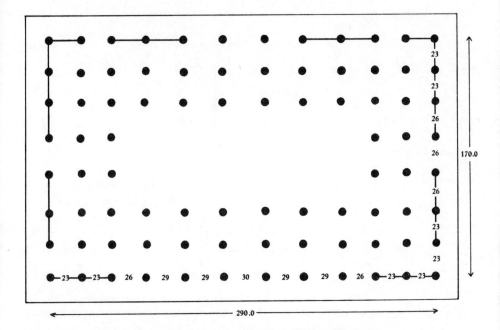

was moved from the Tōdai-ji and rebuilt on the west side of the temple. Behind the Lecture Hall are the stone bases for the columns of the refectory and to the west of these is another set of bases for a smaller building.

As though the Tōdai-ji were not enough, the Saidai-ji seems to have been one last effort to stay abreast of the T'ang style, in this case the elaborate ornamentation of buildings. This West Great Temple was also intended to outshine Shōmu's East Great Temple, the Tōdai-ji. Little of the Saidai-ji remains today, so it is from early texts that one hears about it, and always in superlative terms by the writers. It had two five-storey pagodas, a magnificently ornamented Main Hall, gilt bird and animal finials along the roof lines and rafter-end plaques of Three-colour ware.

Construction was first started on a pair of octagonal seven-storey pagodas, in Chinese style, but the temple archives say the project was abandoned about half way through. For whatever reason, excavations in 1955 verified that the attempt had been made: a large octagonal hole 27 m. across was located. It contained a scattering of special stones of the sort used for the ornamental facing of buildings. Some 88 m. to the west was another tamped earth area, where the other one should have first stood.[28] The platform for the later, east pagoda is intact today. The present Main Hall is a Shaka Hall; it was erected in 1752.

PROVINCIAL TEMPLES

When Emperor Temmu was trying to regain his health in 686 he asked all the provinces to build 'Buddha houses' and to supply them with statues and sūtras. Edicts to provinces to read and copy sūtras had in fact started as early as 677: Jitō issued many such. However, these were only preludes to the real pressure that started in 737 and mounted with the years: edicts went out to make a Shaka and attendants; to make a 7 ft Kannon (740); to make seven Yakushi statues (745); and the nunneries should make a 16 ft Amida (761).

Shōmu demanded of each province a seven-storey pagoda in 740, as a repository for the Konkōmyō-saishō-ō (realm protecting) sūtra. Following on the heels of the smallpox plague that wiped out the four Fujiwara leaders, a reasonable suspicion is that the order hinged on the desire for wider supplication to the deities and respite from the curse. In the next year they received the order for which they had been primed, and probably dreaded—to build temples. A nunnery was also required, to be erected within earshot of the monastery's bell and an easy walk and return within half a day. The late eleventh century *Ruijū-sandai-kyaku* is the document which says that Shōmu transmitted the order in the 3rd month of the 13th year of Tempyō (741), but the Shoku Nihongi credits the inspiration for the order to Empress Kōmyō. Considering her Fujiwara background and their losses, this is quite credible.

Residual resistance to central control was an acknowledged fact in the provinces. The repeated orders suggest that local enthusiasm did not meet the court's expectations. After the completion of the Tōdai-ji, the Provincial Temples (*kokubun-ji*) received more attention, perhaps in the form of direct help through workmen dispatched to outer parts of the country; there is no particular reason to think that the most remote areas were not still ignorant of advanced construction methods. A Buddhist supervisor (*kokushi*) was sent to each province in 744; he operated out of the Provincial Temple. A 747 order provided more paddy-field land for both monasteries and nunneries, but was uncompromising in setting the deadline for the completion of the temples three years later. There were other edicts, donations and more land, and the deadline was probably met. Instructions in 767 to make repairs implies that the temples had been through more than a decade of normal use.

One is justified, however, in asking if the provinces did actually finish the work required of them by building their seven-storey pagodas. None of these temples has any original buildings left and some have been entirely abandoned. A Yakushi Hall stands at a few, but it rarely houses a statue of the eighth century. All the statistics—twenty monks to a monastery, ten nuns to a nunnery, the same number of statues, sūtras, fields, sheaves of rice, and even the same map—lead one to suppose that each temple followed a single model. Ishida assumed that the more detailed information as to how to proceed was probably issued from the Tōdai-ji, and the Tōdai-ji itself may have been the model. He set up an ideal scheme for laying out such a temple, based on a grid in which the South Gate, Middle Gate, Main Hall and Lecture Hall lay along the central north-south axis on the east-west junctures and the first or second rectangles on the second line to the east or west were reserved for the pagoda.[29] Excavations at a number of sites of Provincial Temples have

Fig. 54

Fig. 54 Theoretical scheme of Mosaku Ishida for plans of Provincial Temples, indicating strict south–north sequence of all buildings but pagoda which was flexibly placed to east or west

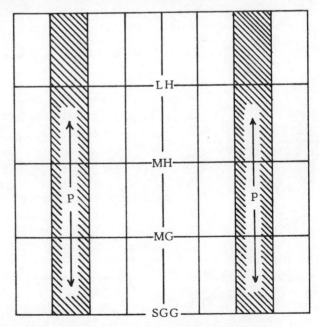

shown that this plan is common but not consistent; moreover, there is far more variety than had been expected. It now appears that in some cases a local temple under construction was converted to a Provincial Temple, and styles older than the eighth century also show up in the provinces. The Hitachi (Ibaragi prefecture) temple may have been in the Kudara Style; the large Sagami (Kanagawa) temple, the Shimōsa (Chiba), Inaba (Tottori) and Hizen (Nagasaki) temples were in the Hōryū-ji Style. The Kai (Yamanashi) and Sanuki (Kagawa) temples appear to have been in the Yakushi-ji plan, less one pagoda. The conventional arrangement, then, saw the Main Hall and a Lecture Hall of about equal size aligned on an axis with the two gates. All the temples seem to have been slightly off the true north line, usually a few degrees to the east.

Fig. 55

Fig. 55   Plans of (left) Rikuzen Provincial Temple, in Sendai city, Miyagi prefecture; mid-eighth century; and (right) Kōka-dera, in Mikumo village, Kōsai-chō, Koga county, Shiga prefecture; eighth century

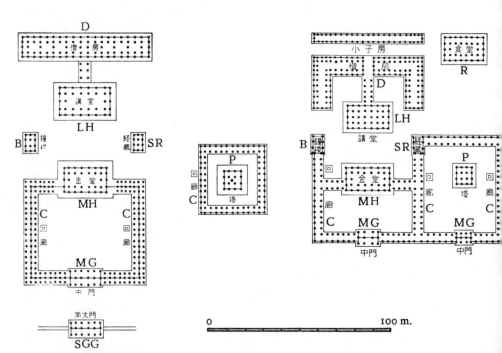

100 m.

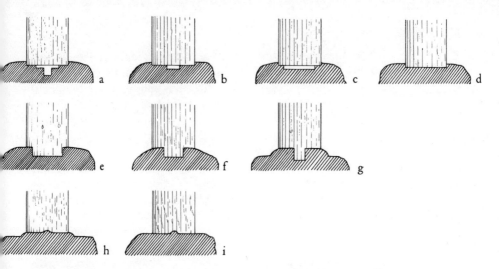

Fig. 56 Types of stone bases for centre poles of pagodas. Distributions are generally as follows: (a) Kinki; (b), (c) Kinki and Kyushu; (d) north and northwest Honshu, Kantō, South Chūbu and Kyushu; (e) widespread; (f) Tōhoku and Inland Sea; (g) chiefly Kantō; (h) Kinki, south Chūbu and Shikoku; (i) Kinki

The centre pole stones were usually shaped and give an interesting history of the development of this facet of the architecture. Buildings still had numerous natural stones for columns as a whole, but more shaping always took place in the Kansai. The centre pole could be inserted into a hollow in the stone or fitted over a raised spot. The early, socketed system often left room below for the relics, as at the Hōryū-ji and Yakushi-ji. This hole was finally dispensed with entirely and a tenoned system was developed, with a medium sized to small hole in the surface of a roughly flattened stone, or small hole in a rounded step. Such a system was unusually prone to rotting, a condition that was considerably improved by raising the pole above the stone. This was done with a step and nipple, or nipple only.

Plate 41

Plates 39, 40

Fig. 56
Plate 52

Most of the Provincial Temples were erected in what was the early tenon stage, and about half were constructed with a stepped base stone with nipple. The changes resulted from the modifications in use of the pagoda, when all need for the relic space had gone, and from more experience in building and technical improvements.

The deterioration of the Nara legal system brought on the eventual passing of the Provincial Temples. A certain amount of reconstruction took place in the Kamakura period with conversion to new sects, retaining the name in tradition only. As early as the ninth century the number had started to dwindle. 'Divine fires' destroyed the Sagami, Tōtōmi, Hida and Izu temples in 819; the Musashi and Kai temples and the Izu nunnery went up in flames in 835, and many storehouses connected with temples were burned. These events were too frequent and too coincidental with the attacks on provincial offices by discon⁄tented local nobles, supported by peasants who were out to ransack the government's granaries, not to have been directly related.³⁰

All told, approximately 120 of these temples were built, but little is known about the nunneries either textually or archaeologically. They were smaller and simpler, although two even had pagodas: Kii (Waka⁄yama) and Izu (Shizuoka). This is probably because they were originally small existing temples which were transformed to comply with the order. The ground plans are recognizable for only about one⁄fourth of the temples today and, in fact, only recently has the identification of all the sites of the Provincial Temples been regarded as accurate. All of the identified temples and monasteries have been designated historic sites.

CHAPTER VIII

Burial Practices and the Cult of Relics

By and large, an over-all reduction in the sizes of mounded tombs after the fifth century reflected the drain on centralized Yamato power that had been brought about by the newly-revived ambitions of regional rulers. Few tombs could match the Kansai ones in scale, but some very large tombs indeed were built, notably in Okayama in the Inland Sea and in outer prefectures of the Kantō plain. By the sixth century, however, a greater number of round tumuli were constructed; others were gourd-shaped. Some of the round tombs were raised over a square base which, like Ishibutai in the Asuka region, had banks reinforced with stones. Yet, despite the reduction in size, the total expense may not have been much less, since most sixth century tombs contained a stone passageway and one or more chambers, following a form that had been brought over from Korea; and constant improvements in the quality of masonry in no way diminished the heavy financial burden and could hardly have shortened the time involved in preparing the tomb. Stone sarcophagi were sometimes included, either in the chamber or passageway.

While the regulations issued in 646 presumably took effect quite rapidly in the Home Provinces, it is apparent that no impact was registered in distant places until some time later. Mounded tombs were still very much in style perhaps as late as the eighth century.

Prince Shōtoku is buried in a tumulus at the foot of Mt Shinaga. This is a spot he is said to have selected himself while out riding on a horse given him by his friend Hata Kawakatsu, when looking for temple sites and a place for his tomb. At least, so say the archives of the Eifuku-ji, the temple built in front of his mound. The prince was only twenty-seven when he picked out the place, but some twenty years later he returned and allowed the local people to start work on the tomb. He died in Ikaruga at the age of forty-nine.

Empress Suiko is supposed to have ordered the building of a temple at the site as a memorial, but it took a dramatic revival of interest in the prince and the rise of a cult in the Kamakura period for the Eifuku-ji to come into its own. There may now be seen a Tokugawa-style structure at the entrance to the tomb, and no claims are made by the temple for

Fig. 16

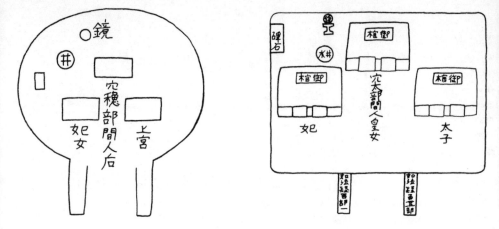

Fig. 57 Sketches of the tomb of Prince Shōtoku (left) from an undated manuscript in Eifuku-ji written after the tomb had been looted; and (right) from a manuscript in the temple of the late seventeenth century, after a description of the tomb by Jōjō who claimed to have entered it

Plate 55

greater antiquity than the Kamakura period of other buildings and furnishings. A scroll illustrating the life of priest Ippen painted at the end of the thirteenth century shows a tree-covered mound with a small building in front and part of a walled enclosure, but has few other embellishments. The present mound is 7 m. high and 54 m. in diameter.

Several things are certain about the prince's tomb. His mother died in 621; the prince and his wife both died a year later and were placed in the same tomb chamber. The tomb is commonly believed to have been looted in the middle ages and a 1349 record based on popular opinion says that the body of the prince was destroyed and everything, such as the gold dust, had been stolen. The chamber may have stood open for a long time after the looting, but probably was closed to the public by the Kamakura period. At least when the priest Jōjō entered the tomb he had to do so surreptitiously.

Jōjō's information contradicts the earlier record, but this is not to say that the tomb could not have been refurnished at the time the prince was being resanctified. According to Jōjō, in front of the three sarcophagi stood a pair of 'red copper' lions; on the left side of the chamber was a well with good tasting water; on the wall behind it hung a mirror, and against the left wall stood a stone epitaph written by Kōbō Daishi (*d.*

835). He listed the measurements of the coffins and said that inside each
was an intact brocade on which lay a skeleton. All the physical remains
looked alike. There was a strange odour about the place. At the front
were wall niches that contained 100 copies of the Lotus Sūtra on one
side and 125 on the other. On the basis of this description a schematic
layout of the interior of the tomb was drawn up in a temple document   *Fig. 57*
showing a sarcophagus near the back wall and two farther forward and
on either side, but the only thing to commend the diagram is the relative
position of the interior equipment. The latitudinal shape is quite
impossible.

The Imperial Office made its own report in 1879 when repairs were
carried out on the tomb, and it included fairly exact measurements but
without illustrations. There was a passageway 24 ft long, 6 ft wide and
6 ft high, and a main chamber 18 ft deep, 10 ft wide and 10 ft high. The
passage was built of four large stones on either side and three overhead;
the chamber had five stones in each side wall, two in the back wall and
two overhead. Three large, carefully cut stone blocks lay on the floor.
The centre block at the back was hollowed out to a depth of about 9 ins;
this depression sloped down to drainage holes at either end. The block
measured 6.6 ft long, 2.5 wide and 1.6 high. Presumably it held the
coffin of Prince Shōtoku's mother, or she was laid directly in the
depression. The one on the right measured 8 by 3.65 by 2.2 ft, and the
one on the left 7.15 by 3 by 2.2 ft. These two apparently held the remains
of the prince and his wife. Piles of pieces of black dry lacquer lay near
the blocks; these may have been the debris of the sarcophagi. The
investigators saw no well.

Umehara noted the unusual similarity between the description of this
tomb and the Iwayayama Tomb, and reconstructed the prince's   *Plates 59, 60*
passageway and chamber on the basis of Iwayayama, which is probably
datable to the early seventh century. He did not agree entirely with the
Imperial Office's report which raised serious doubts over the many
discrepancies between Jōjō's statements and earlier accounts and regarded
his information as having simply incorporated current temple legends.
There is considerable uncertainty as to whether he had even entered the
tomb. In effect, Jōjō was making his own, perhaps unsolicited, contribution to the Prince Shōtoku cult. In glossy language, even the foul
smell became only a strange odour, but, as Umehara points out, the

dimensions for the blocks given by the priest are too accurate to be pure guesswork: back block: 6.5 by 3 by 1.5 ft; right block: 8 by 3.7 by 2 ft; left block: 7.2 by 3 by 1.7 ft.[1] Incidentally, everyone agrees that Prince Shōtoku was a man of considerable stature, but few have sug gested that his wife was a woman of formidable dimensions. Archaeo logically speaking, Umehara thought it was clear that the hollowed out block at the back was contemporaneous with the construction of the tomb, while the two with flat surfaces were moved in later.

There is ample textual information on co burials that is often bolstered by archaeological evidence. One item comes from the seventh century Shōgakusan mounds in Kashiwara city of Osaka prefecture where a cluster of eight tombs includes five that are precisely aligned. A bronze grave marker, recovered long ago, bears the name of Funashi Ōgo Obito—a name connected with a prosperous shipping family. Among other things, it says that he built his mound beside that of his elder brother. Because of his recognized abilities he was promoted to one of the highest ranks; he died in 641 and was buried with his wife, but not until 688. This astonishing span of forty seven years has been called either an error or an unexpected delay in the construction of the tomb. Such leisurely interments are otherwise unprecedented; for instance, in what is in itself a rare occurrence, Emperor Kimmei was buried about six years after his death; emperors Jomei and Temmu were both buried a little over a year after they had died. Neither explanation may be correct. Funashi Ōgo Obito was probably reburied when his wife died,[2] in an addition to the family or ancestral tombs. The inscription concludes with the wish that the place be a safe one, protected for ten thousand generations as a hallowed spot for the clan.

In the long run, Buddhist burials were incompatible with the pomp and ostentation of the mounded tombs, but the proscription against mound building was already taking its toll by the time of the first official notice concerning cremation. Even the wealthiest of families could hardly afford the expense of building both temples and tombs, and a practical observation opens the section of the edict that deals with burials by lamenting the poverty of the country as due to the practice of erecting expensive tombs. Following tradition, however, many later emperors were buried in or on mounds—if only modest ones— even after cremation of their remains became fashionable.

Medium to large sized tumuli in the fifth century were usually built on a plain, but in the following century there was a tendency to construct more frequently on a hillside or to tunnel into it. There are many clusters of the latter cave-style tombs hollowed out of appropriate cliff-sides ranging geographically from Kyushu to the Kantō. In the south these may be cut into rock and reproduce the corridor and chamber of con-structed tombs; in the Kantō they are dug into the hard loam, but still reproduce—though in a more general way—the internal features of a mounded tomb.

With a total depth of rarely more than 15 ft, there is a low narrow corridor which opens out into a vault-shaped, rectangular chamber floored with stones, only wide enough for bodies to be stretched out laterally. Rock-cut tombs may have sill-like dividers to separate two or more bodies laid out the length of the chamber. These tombs were rarely designed to hold the remains of more than three people.

The time span is quite considerable between the earliest of these rock-cut tombs in Kyushu and the latest in the Kantō; it may be four or more centuries, thereby suggesting a date for the latter as recent as the tenth century. Archaeologists accept them as burials for members of the upper class and, if nothing else, they point up the fact that cremation made slow progress even in some well populated parts of the country.

By way of example, four tombs were investigated by International Christian University near the university campus in Mitaka city, a suburb of west Tokyo, which were discovered by workmen who were terracing the hillside for the construction of two houses in 1964. Popu-larly called *yokoana*, horizontal holes, these had been cut into the loam on two slightly different levels, about 12 m. up the slope above the little river called Nogawa. They were dug into a rounded contour of the hillside. Many similar clusters of tunnel tombs have been discovered over the years along this bluff that runs for many miles beside a wide ancient river bed, the remains of which show up as the Musashino gravel layer.

The largest tomb was in excellent condition, with its walls intact. The narrow vault-shaped passageway was closed by a pile of smooth fist-sized pebbles. The chamber was 225 cm. in length, 152 cm. in height at the front and 210 cm. at the back. Most of the floor was laid with a single layer of pebbles, but this had been thickened at the back where the bodies

Plate 61

Plate 63

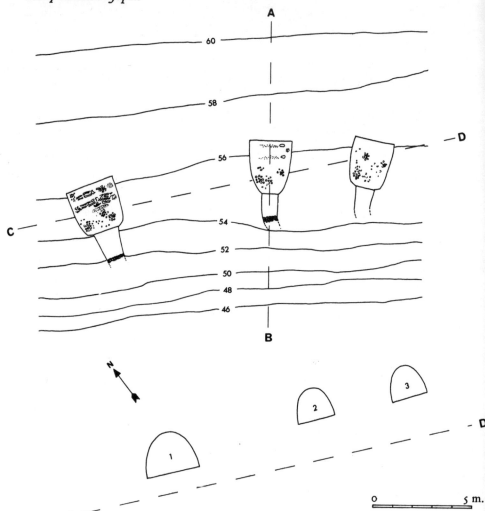

Fig. 58a   Plan and section CD of three of the four tunnel tombs discovered in Ōsawa, Mitaka city, Tokyo. Probably tenth century

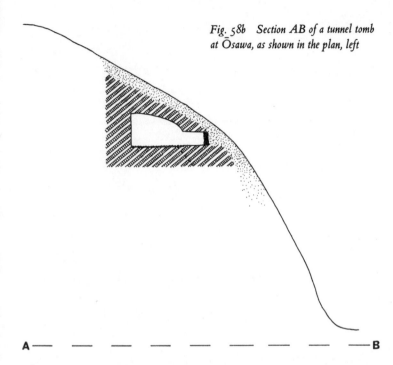

Fig. 58b   Section AB of a tunnel tomb at Ōsawa, as shown in the plan, left

A—— —— —— —— —— —— —— —— ——B

were placed. The skeletons were preserved, since they were not in direct contact with the soil. One, a female, lay near the back wall. Its extended length on the ground was 176 cm. Beside her lay a male skeleton, with an extended length of 183 cm; and beside him the bones of a child reduced to powder; only two milk teeth could be recovered.

The second tomb was higher on the hillside and in softer loam. Its passageway was curved, as was also the passageway of the third tomb. Part of the vault had collapsed, causing extensive disintegration of the skeletal materials. The remaining bones, consisting of two partial skulls and fragments perhaps belonging to a third individual, were in great disarray. The culprit was apparently a raccoon-dog; its jaw bone was found in the middle of the floor. It had worked its way in and scattered the remains before it died. The entrance was only half plugged with stones; the uneven floor consisted of stones of less uniform sizes than in the first tomb.

Fig. 58

The third tomb had a poorly laid floor and looked unfinished. No stones closing the entrance could be found. Large sections of the walls had peeled off and only one small fragment of a bone was located. On the west side of the back wall and on the adjoining side wall were deep incised markings, but no clear patterns or order were apparent; some parallel and curved lines had vague floral shapes.

Plate 62

A fourth tunnel tomb was dug out several months later by workmen putting in a septic tank. Its passageway yielded a Sue vase, the only item of this sort that came from any of the tombs and the chief local clue to their dating. It is here believed to be about the tenth century. Other cases of the ceremonial deposit of a single vase or plate show that grave-goods were symbolically indicated in this way fairly frequently in this area at the time. One of these tombs, located several miles farther along the bluff, investigated after having been opened by workmen who were digging a well in 1959, yielded only one small blue glass bead, which was probably a costume ornament. This particular tomb lay under a private house. The fairly well preserved bones had to be removed to a temple before nightfall at the insistence of the resident, and later properly interred.

CREMATIONS

The cremation of priest Dōshō is regarded as the official beginning of the practice. Dōshō was cremated at his request by his followers in the year 700. There is a rather long description in the Shoku Nihongi for the 10th day of the 3rd month of the 4th year of Emperor Mommu's reign which tells of the priest's background, his trip to China and tutelage under Hsüan-tsang, his return and service at the Gankō-ji (he founded the Hossō sect), his construction of bridges and ferry boats and his death at the age of seventy-two. Dōshō's disciples carried out his will and cremated his remains at Kurihara, but they immediately fell to fighting between themselves and his relatives over the disposition of his ashes. The issue resolved itself when a sudden wind blew the ashes away! None were ever recovered.

Fig. 59

The Shoku Nihongi was attempting to pin-point the beginning of cremation in Japan, but there is archaeological evidence that it was not the first time that it had happened.[3] There are even Buddhist motifs in mounded tombs, such as the lotus flower patterns on either end of the lid of one of the two stone sarcophagi in the Midoro Tomb in Nara

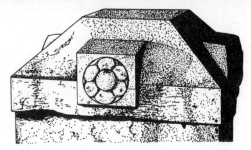

Fig. 59 Lotus carved on lid of stone sarcophagus in Midoro Tomb, Katsura village, Minami-katsuragi county, Nara prefecture, said to be the tomb of Soga no Iruka who died in 645

prefecture, and a pair of lotuses on one end of a clay sarcophagus from the Honbōzan Tomb in Okayama prefecture.

'Cremation mounds' of about the late sixth century have been identified, ten of which were reported by 1967.[4] While these are concentrated in Osaka, they are also found east to Shizuoka and west to Hyōgo. Interestingly enough, none is mentioned for the Kyoto-Nara area. Most of these tombs are not far from Sue pottery kilns. They are small, low mounds, averaging 15 m. in diameter and no more than 3 m. in height, if there is even a mound at all. One in the Hijiri Shrine grounds, Izumi city, Osaka prefecture, had four coffins but a total of eight people. The only one reported from Shiga prefecture contained four wooden coffins which had been later buried near the top of the mound. The number of individuals cremated inside could not be determined.

A slanted wooden frame resembling the walls and roof of a simple house was raised over a rectangular hole and the floor was paved with pebbles. This frame was mounded over with earth, and coffins, or sometimes just bodies, were placed inside and grave-goods around. Fire was started in a pit; a vent allowed smoke to escape. Everything of wood was destroyed by the fire, which also hardened the interior surfaces and tended to bake an overhead vault in place.

The Akogashima 10 tomb, Shizuoka, was moated and had a very short corridor leading into a main chamber, the latter 3.60 by 2.10 m. in size. Many post-holes around the outer edge of the rectangular hole of the main chamber held the sloping supports for the rafters of the structure.

The grave-goods recovered from these tombs are typical enough for the Late Tomb period: iron swords, knives, sickles and nails; various kinds of horse trappings; belt buckles, ear-rings in all but one tomb, beads of stone and glass, and Sue pottery almost throughout. One tomb in Osaka contained some Haji pottery.

Needless to say, it may be argued that these are not Buddhist incin, erations, since Buddhist burials are commonly recognized by the criteria of three stages: cremation, storing of ashes in a container, and eventual burial of the container. This common conception of the Buddhist burial may well be of only its most sophisticated form and primarily of that indulged in by some of the nobility of the Kyoto-Nara area, clergy and royalty. Who else but Buddhists in Japan at that time would have wanted to follow the cremation practice, it is difficult to imagine. Perhaps best here is to regard these tombs as in the incipient stage of Buddhist cremation in Japan.

The Shoku Nihongi says that Empress Jitō was cremated at Asuka no Oka in Taihō 3, 12th month, 17th day (704), and buried on the 26th day at Ōuchi no Sanryō. She had died almost exactly a year earlier. This is the mound that today goes by the name of Hinokuma Ōuchi no

Plate 64

Misasagi (or ryō), and is the tomb said to be that of Emperor Temmu. Pilferers entered it in 1235 by cutting a narrow hole through the south, stone door. In a record, *Aoki no Sanryōki*, drawn up shortly after the looting was discovered, the interior of the tomb is described as an antechamber and main chamber made of granite with perfectly fitting stones, with a ceiling about 7 ft high. The walls and ceiling are painted red; a swinging gilt bronze door closed the entrance of the main chamber. Temmu's sarcophagus is of red lacquered cloth (dry lacquer), laid on a gilt bronze platform. There is a red cloth inside the coffin. The record even gives the length of some of the long bones; his head was abnormally large and was red (painted?) and black. Lying beside the sarcophagus was a gilt bronze bowl that held a silver bone or ash container. The grave, goods included a belt with jade ornament, beads of amber and a drum, shaped pillow decorated with gold, silver and beads, which seemed to the writers of the report to be Chinese. The objects scattered around the tomb and not stolen were moved to the Tachibana-dera, the temple nearby.

Since the time of this document it has been widely accepted that Jitō's remains were in the silver container in the bowl alongside Temmu's sarcophagus. The looting, which inspired the report, inadvertently provided the evidence for full acceptance of the Shoku Nihongi's description of Jitō's cremation.

Cremation spread through the upper classes after it was sanctioned by royal adoption, then proceeded down the social ladder. Through directions given in the Yōrō Civil Code, it is clear that the government came to regard cremation as necessary for hygienic reasons. A soldier who died while on duty, either in battle or otherwise, and the unclaimed bodies of civil employees were to be cremated on the spot.[5] Ordinarily, incineration was carried out at a kiln or at the burial site itself. When the practice took on a uniquely Buddhist relationship, among those who could afford it, the ashes were put in one or more containers and placed in some kind of a small, perhaps natural, mound with a stone marker, a small stone pagoda, a wooden tablet, or some other indicator. Preference was shown for burials near hills, at the foot of a slope or on higher ground and, in the majority of cases, close to the spot the individual regarded as 'home.'

Cremation seems to be alluded to metaphorically in eighth century poetry. The Manyōshū contains several remarks on lost loved ones taking the form of clouds floating away, and in some cases drifting in the direction of sacred mountains. These have been taken as oblique references to cremation[6] and are made more credible by the inclusion of known cremation sites such as Yoshinoyama and Hatsuseyama. Two examples may be given by way of illustration:

> *The cloud drifting over the brows*
> *Of the hills of secluded Hatsusé—*
> *Can it, alas, be she?* (III: 428)

> *Yesterday he lived here,*
> *But unexpectedly*
> *He hovers now in clouds*
> *Above the sea-beach pines.* (III: 444)[7]

With relatively insignificant marking, the existence of the burials was as often as not gradually forgotten. One of the best examples of this is the discovery of the cinerary urn of Ina no Mabito Ōmura, an individual mentioned in the Shoku Nihongi, by a farmer in the eighteenth century when he was cultivating his land at Anamushiyama in Nara prefecture. It is a gilt bronze globular container said to have been in a large jar; inside was a small wooden box containing bone-ash. The inscription of 392 characters on the bronze container tells the life history of the man, his rank, his appointment as head of the Echigo castle, his death two years

Plate 66

later (707) at the age of forty-six and the return of his bones for burial at the foot of Mt Nijō.

Bronze vessels were most often used as containers for ashes in the early eighth century when well-to-do priests or those who could acquire foreign articles were initiating the practice. Other materials for cinerary urns were stone, lacquer, glass, wood, Haji, Sue and Three-colour pottery. Unglazed vessels increased in popularity through the eighth and into the ninth century, and especially in outlying areas as people of lesser rank took up the practice.

Fig. 60

Early cinerary urns of pottery tended to be copies of the standard bronze shape. A globular shape was the most common, although a fair number of bowls, boxes and other shapes have been found. Box-shaped bone containers come only in bronze, wood or stone.

Epitaphs associated with these burials provide valuable information, usually identifying the person and his occupation by means of references to his appointments and rank, and giving the date of his death. A number of Wadō-kaichin, Ryūhei-eihō and Jingō-kaihō coins have been found with these burials, and help to furnish relative dates, but few grave-goods normally come up with cremations except for an occasional sword and costume and body ornaments.

Plates 67, 68

The written information is supplied on a rectangular tablet (often in its own box) or directly on the vessel itself. In most cases the tablet is bronze or gilt bronze, but a rare silver one has been recovered, as have several examples in stone. The dates on these epitaphs (of which more than a dozen are known) range only between 707 and 784; none have been found outside the Kansai. They are, in other words, the hallmark of the small, literate, upper class living in the Home Provinces, who had access to the materials and were in touch with the Chinese practice of recording the life history of the deceased. The disappearance of the epitaphs is further testimony to the spread of this burial system to those with lower levels of literacy and with lesser means.

RELICS, PAGODAS AND MOUNDS

An early elaboration of this practice was performed by monks who wanted to emulate the custom of depositing relics of Buddha or a sainted

Fig. 60   Stone urn for ashes, with cover, from Egawa, Kisarazu city, Chiba prefecture. Height of box 17.5 cm. Eighth century

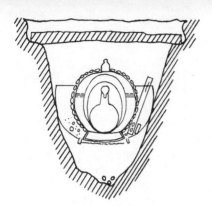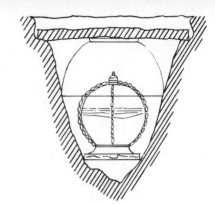

Fig. 61   Relics in hole of base stone of centre pole of pagoda of Hōryū-ji (left) as discovered in 1949; and (right) as they were probably deposited in the late seventh century as restored by Ishida, resting on the mirror and covered by the gilt bronze bowl

personage at a spot accessible to pilgrims for veneration. Bones were sometimes put into a glass bottle or silver container and then in a bronze vessel that was sealed inside a wooden or stone box. In this *busshari* practice, as the Japanese call it—the burial of Buddhist relics—the individual would be less likely to command the valuable collection that a temple might have, which by the end of the seventh century had come to look more suitable for such use than the secular array of Tomb period objects unearthed from the site of the Asuka-dera's pagoda. The 1949 repairs of the Hōryū-ji, for instance, gave an opportunity for the relics to be removed, copied and replaced. They were all within a gilt bronze basin which had been lodged in a tapered hole in the base stone, the top of the hole then covered by a stone slab. A few small bells had found

Fig. 61

Fig. 62   Two inner containers with hinged lids for relics of the pagoda of Hōryū-ji; (left) silver, height 9.8 cm.; and (right) gold, height 8.1 cm.

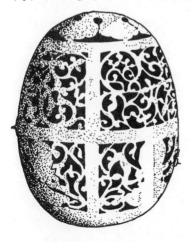

their way into the bottom of the hole. In the basin was a Chinese 'white copper' Lion and Grape mirror, too large (10.2 cm. in diameter) to go into any other receptacle, that should date to the end of the seventh century or the beginning of the eighth, and some small bells and beads. A bronze container holding a number of beads rested in this bowl. Inside it were two egg-shaped, openwork containers, one within the other, the larger one of silver, the smaller of gold. Their decoration consists of stylized floral patterns. Within this was a glass bottle with silver stopper. All told, there were 272 glass beads, 627 pearls, one gold bar, one ivory tubular bead, one pearl shell and one piece each of crystal, amber, calcite and incense wood.

Fig. 62

Another example is the relics from an abandoned temple called Mishima-hai-ji (hai = abandoned), at Oda in Ibaragi city, Osaka prefecture, now kept in the National Museum in Tokyo. These were extracted in 1907 from a hole in the stone base for the pagoda's centre pole. A lidded, soft limestone chest 20.3 cm. in length contained a bronze jar; this jar held a small bronze box about 2.5 by 4 cm. and this in turn held a tiny gold reliquary box about 1.5 by 0.7 cm.

The *raison d'être* of the pagoda had been re-appraised by the middle of the eighth century, and after the introduction of the twin pagodas the temples were hard put to find a use for the second one. Buried relics, or occasionally relics installed in the spire, came to be replaced by sūtras. This was, for instance, the purpose for building the pagodas of the Provincial Temples, as ordered by Emperor Shōmu. In effect, then, the second pagoda of a temple was little more than ornamental. The sūtra mounds of later centuries are indirectly related to this transposition that saw holy writ elevated to a new status, and may even suggest some response to the depleting reservoir of relics.

The burial of sūtras in mounds was introduced to Japan by the Tendai priest Jikaku Taishi after his return from China in 847. The oldest dated mound, however, is no earlier than 1007, and is a mound erected by Fujiwara Dōchō on Kimpusen in the Yoshino region[8] where, incidentally, numerous mounds exist. The practice lasted well into the Edo period. It spread throughout the country, leaving major concentrations in the Kinki, Kantō and in north Kyushu. It is not by accident that many mounds or groups of mounds were built in mountainous areas marked by holy Shinto spots.

Fig. 63

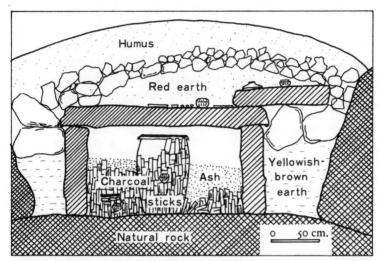

Fig. 63   Section of Sūtra mound number 3, at Kamikurayama, Shingū, Wakayama prefecture. The flat stones held two bronze mirrors of Japanese make, small iron swords, an upside down yellow-glazed dish, and two small globular jars, one without a lid. The large clay pot contained another small globular jar, set in with sticks of charcoal, and was covered by a large Chinese bronze mirror. A Japanese bronze mirror and two more small globular jars were among the charcoal sticks inside the cistic formation. c. eleventh century

The early buried sūtras were written on paper, engraved on copper plate, scratched on tile or pieces of talc. Later ones, deposited when reasons for burial had changed and less expensive materials were used, were inscribed on wood or consisted of merely a magical symbol (borrowed from sanskrit) on a stone or shell.

The sūtras chosen for burial were primarily those used by the Tendai sect, and were often accompanied by a selection of bronze mirrors, swords, arrow-heads, knives, ritual paraphernalia, small images and coins. Early mounds usually contain a little globular vessel (*gosu*). Mirrors and knives were believed to protect the sūtra from the evil forces that were attempting to destroy it.[9] Other associated things, particularly of later centuries, were of a more personal nature, such as fans, combs, eyebrow paint, rouge and small Chinese porcelain lidded jars that were probably used as white powder containers. The mirrors, in a variety of kinds and even earlier dates, were often engraved with Buddhist figures on the reflecting surface, one of the most popular subjects being Amida Buddha.

Most mounds did not exceed 2 m. in height and 10 m. in diameter. Some were marked with little stone stūpas. The sūtra was put into a cylindrical metal or stone container and, in the early centuries of the practice, was placed in a small stone chamber within the mound along with the accompanying articles.

By the late tenth century it was widely believed that the End of the Law (Mappō) would take place in 1052, after which the protective power of the Buddha would wane and even the entire scripture might eventually disappear. To cope with this contingency, sūtras were buried in mounds to await the coming of Miroku, the Buddha of the Future. But as realization slowly dawned that Mappō had failed to materialize, the nature of the practice changed and sūtras were interred as memorials, to await rebirth in the land of bliss, or for other, very often mundane, reasons.

Fig. 64

Pagodas represent all levels of status and ambition, from a building for an aristocrat's temple to a miniature clay model for an ardent Buddhist of lower standing. Many sizes and varieties are known in both stone and pottery, some clearly indicating the place of origin of the user. Almost inevitably, sharper lines are drawn in the burial customs between foreign and native practitioners; it is through the sorting and adapting process that the Japanese preference makes itself known. A five-storeyed pottery pagoda about 6 ft high was excavated from a site in west Tokyo. There must have been more of these and undoubtedly scores of other smaller ones from early centuries that have long since disappeared, but a mini-

Fig. 65

ature pagoda is among the Three-colour wares in the Shōsōin, part of the possessions of the pious Emperor Shōmu. Its movable roofs slip on over a centre pin.

Plate 71

Stone pagodas can be seen in stone reliefs, carved out of rock in free-standing form, and constructed. The total number of extant early examples is not many, but within this group each type points up a variety of areas of origin and the influences that were converging on Japan. The Ishidō-ji, in an isolated spot in Shiga prefecture, is believed to be the work of new arrivals from Paekche around 669 on the basis of a reference in the Nihon Shoki to 700 Koreans settling in Gamō in Ōmi province. The broad, unbroken walls and flat roofs for each storey, along with the proportionally tall spire, are little modified from its Korean prototypes; but it is a shape that met with very limited acceptance in Japan.

Fig. 64 Brown pottery pagoda model, from Mawarida, Higashi-murayama-chō, Kitatama county, Tokyo. Height 196.5 cm.; late eighth century. National Museum, Tokyo

Fig. 65 Three-colour pottery pagoda model, roofs in alternate colours of green and yellowish-brown made separately and held by a metal pin, in Shōsōin, Nara city. Height 17.2 cm. Mid-eighth century

The popularity as a burial ground of Ashoka-ōzan, as the place is called, developed after esoteric practices brought in the use of *gorintō*, the five-tiered stone stūpas. There are thousands of these little stūpas here, on the platform supporting the three-storeyed pagoda, on terraces outside the walk surrounding the platform, and slightly lower on the hill top. Small stones with figures carved in relief are also of a later date.

The thirteen-storeyed pagoda of the Rokutani-ji, carved out of the tufa summit of a lower but steep hill on the west side of Mt Nijō, may be said to represent an idea that was ultimately Indian in its rock-cut technique, but, at this stage, perhaps more Chinese in its tapered shape. Although not far above the present road that crosses the mountain, the path follows the sheer rock in some places. The geological formation lent itself to the hacking out of a pagoda, grotto and stone surfaces for reliefs. The pagoda is solid; only its cap is missing. One small hole about a foot deep, intended for bones or ashes, appears at the top of the base, and one, which may have been made later, on the east side on the fifth storey level. In the shallow grotto nearby is a flat wall surface bearing three engraved Buddhas, each with different hand gestures, in the Late Asuka or Nara period style. Buddhas carved out of the side of the rock elsewhere are badly weathered or damaged, almost beyond recognition.

The main part of the temple site down the hill to the west has been excavated. Its residential area yielded some Sue and Haji pottery of the Nara period and a Wadō-kaichin coin.

An unusual stone structure that may be a kind of stūpa with which a group of monks wanted their ashes to be associated, stands on the summit of Kumayama in a remote spot in Okayama prefecture. Its core is a hole within which was placed a cylinder consisting of a series of joined pottery tubes of the Sue type, capped with a bullet-shaped top. Inside was a small globular container of Three-colour ware. The superstructure was erected on a square platform in two levels and given a rectangular niche on each lower side and a deep square hole running down the middle from the top. The square hole, which measures 70 cm. on each side, is covered by two slabs.

Whatever the, perhaps, locally determined use of the niches—for sūtras, bones, ashes, food, incense, flowers or other offerings—and even the local character of the pottery tube, this structure matches examples in China and is regarded as the work of Chinese immigrants.[10] Presumably

Plate 72

Fig. 66   Sue pottery cylinder, from Kumayama Kaidan, Okayama prefecture. Height 165 cm. Eighth century

the ashes of the monks (or at least ardent Buddhists) were poured into the container to be in as close contact as possible with the reliquary. There would have been little difficulty in removing the cap of the tube to make further additions.

Plate 65

Buddhist sculptures were carved out of natural rock formations along roads or cliffs where associated buildings were sometimes erected, or out of granite or sandstone for use outdoors at sacred places. One that was moved indoors—at an early date, to judge by the appearance of its surface—is the triad at the Ishii-dera in Nara prefecture, now placed above the altar in the only building of that temple.

Preserved more or less *in situ* on a mound in Nara city called Zutō are thirteen slabs bearing reliefs or engravings. The mound was once within the vast precincts of the Shin-yakushi-ji on a line leading south from the South Great Gate of the Tōdai-ji. The Shin-yakushi-ji has since been scaled down to a single block of dilapidated buildings, and Zutō has for centuries been almost hidden among residences. The information on its initial, relative location comes from the *Tōdai-ji Yōroku*, the ten volume record of the temple completed in 1106, which also says that the chief priest Rōben ordered Jicchū, one of his disciples, to build the stūpa in the year 767 in order to regain peace and to provide protection for the land. There is a good chance, in other words, that its erection was connected with the revolt of Emi no Oshikatsu and the resulting shock the uprising brought to what was believed to be a stable state.

Plates 87, 88

Zutō is a square mound with flattish top, designed for circumambu-lation and ascent. Its carved slabs are situated on four levels and were once set into tiled niches. The tile fragments, incidentally, are similar to those of the Lecture Hall of the Tōdai-ji and verify the records' dating of the monument. Ten of the stones seem to be in their original positions, but the others have been shifted by landslides or by other causes. Perhaps more stones once existed. The open space on the south side has five gorintō, small stūpas of five superimposed symbolic shapes, and several other stones that were added sometime in the thirteenth century.

Fig. 67

The consistency in style and technique, including the engraving on two stones, places all of the slabs in a single time period, but positive identifi-cation of the Buddhas of many of the groups has yet to be established. One might expect the application of an ideal iconographical scheme of Buddhist paradises associated with the four directions; if such a scheme could be shown to exist, it would answer the long-standing question of how far Japanese iconography had advanced by the latter half of the eighth century. The Buddha of the middle group of the lowest level on the west side qualifies as an Amida of the Western Paradise by his hand gestures and a pair of little figures which must be floating on a lotus pond below. On the basis of the mudrā alone, however, the Buddhas on four separate slabs could all be Amida, with hand gestures of appeasement in the case of two and of concentration in the case of two more. By the same standard, four slabs could be Shaka, with the mudrā of preaching (or fearlessness) in the case of three, and earth-touching in the case of one. But the three in the mudrā of fearlessness could also be Yakushi at this stage. Identification may eventually come with the sorting out of the correct combinations of clouds or flowers overhead or building behind, number of figures, hand gestures, standing or variously seated bod-hisattvas, and flowers or little figures below. By eighth century yardsticks for triads and formal groups, it is a rich collection of sculptures. A build-ing shown behind a preaching Shaka (?) has a railing and recessed wall planes like those on the Hōryū-ji's Main Hall and pagoda. Large bells hang from the corners of its eaves.

Plate 87

Plate 88

A rather similar squarish mound called Dotō (Earth tower) is in the grounds of the Ōno-dera in Sakai city, Osaka prefecture. Each side measures about 30 m. at the base. If once terraced, the steps are no longer very well defined and, today at least, there is no stone reinforcing. Unlike Zutō, it has no carved stones decorating its slopes. Many tiles picked up at this stūpa seem to have been donations for the mound's construction. In an unusual harvest of information, quite a number bear inscriptions that include names datable to between 751 and 759, and so furnish an acceptable mid-eighth century date for the erection of the mound.[11]

0   10 m.

CHAPTER IX

Stone Carvings and Monuments

Patently improved stone work is visible in the construction of the chambers of a few of the latest tombs in the Kansai. Examples include the Monjuin Nishi Tomb, Sakurai, and the Iwayayama Tomb south of Kashiwara city. It takes little imagination to see a diversion of this skill and interest to the production of several monuments and, by extension, to the carving of a number of figures which are scattered throughout the southern Asuka countryside.

Carved from granite, in an unsophisticated stage of three-dimensional stone sculpture, they represent an art that lost its continuity once the capital was moved from south Asuka. Few statues are in their original locations and some are today near tombs. But one may conjecture that it was not tombs with which they were originally identified but in some cases with gardens as ornaments of a religious significance and, in other cases, with roads as protectors.

The number of examples is not large. They show an art that lacked sound technical and iconographical traditions. Stylistic consistency is not a salient feature; the forms are ponderous and block-like. There are notations in the Nihon Shoki implying court patronage of at least one aspect of the art, but since almost all the stones are in the Asuka region, it may be assumed that the art as a whole had court approval if not full support.

Tsuboi was intrigued by the number of stone floors in the Asuka region and thought that they might have some mutual connection, pointing out a paved area at the site of the Ishigami Pond, another in front of the south gate of the Asuka-dera, paved floors at the Asuka Itabuki Palace site and at the supposed residence of Soga no Umako (not far from Ishibutai, apparently his huge tomb, now Asuka's most impressive monument). These floors may have been associated with residential or palace grounds and have had some ceremonial use.[1]

Plate 9

The Nihon Shoki records an interesting story that took place during the reign of Empress Saimei. In 656 she ordered the building of a canal from Mt Kagu to Mt Ishigami (it should not have exceeded two km.) to carry stones on barges for the construction of a wall. Two hundred

Fig. 67   South side of Zutō, Buddhist mound, in Kamishimuzu-chō, Nara city.
◀ *Probably 767*

147

barges were required after over 30,000 men had dug the canal. More than 70,000 men worked on the wall. While all of this was being done, which apparently took several months, the wood that had been collected for building the palace rotted. Complaints and recriminations were widespread. One was the frequently voiced hope that the mound constructed at Ishigami would collapse of its own accord.[2] Incidentally, while little evidence of all of this remains today, a small number of large, flat surfaced stones on the hillside above the Asuka-dera, probably connected with this wall, show that either wishful thinking or time had its effect.

The empress, who had extravagant tastes, met her social obligations in grand flourishes. Activities in her reign give some inkling as to what the stacked stones may actually be. Called Shumisen by the Japanese, that is, Mt Meru or Sumeru, the Buddhist holy mountain, one of these stands in the grounds of the National Museum in Tokyo today. It was brought here, along with a stone of paired figures, from the region of the Ishigami Pond where it may have been a garden fixture. Like many other rulers, Empress Saimei enjoyed open-air parties. In the 3rd year of her reign (657), 7th month, 15th day, a model of Mt Sumeru was built to the west of the Asuka-dera; the Obon festival was held and a group of foreigners was entertained. In the 5th year, 3rd month, 17th day, another Mt Sumeru was constructed on the bank of the river east of Amakashi no oka and Emishi (presumably Ainu) from different localities were entertained. Again, in the 6th year, on an unspecified day in the 5th month, a third Mt Sumeru was erected near the pond of Ishigami, this time 'as high as a pagoda.' Forty-seven foreigners were entertained.

No reference is made to the materials used, but the standing monument in the National Museum grounds should be one of the last two mentioned. It was erected, in other words, to commemorate special receptions, and for people regarded as foreigners. Three-piece, disjointed, and resembling a snowman, it bears undulating reliefs simulating rolling mountain ranges not unlike Han dynasty 'hill censers.' The decoration is poorly co-ordinated between levels, and the middle band is in higher relief. One might wish to make a plausible thesis for the monument— and in the process give the sculptors the benefit of the doubt—either being short of one section or being a composite of the better preserved sections

of more than one model of Mt Sumeru. The interior is hollow; it may
have been designed to work like a fountain. When the site was investigated in 1936, a spot about 100 m. north of the Asuka-dera, the area
around the figures was found to be ditched; adjacent to it on the east was
a surface paved with pebbles. On the south was a ditch which may have
served as the overflow; it zigzagged away in a westerly direction. According to the excavators, the plan resembled a water course through a
garden.³

The stone statue standing nearby in the National Museum grounds
may be a *dōso-jin*, a roadside protective deity, of the sort still familiar in
various parts of the country today. The *Fusō Ryakki*, a book of 938,
speaks of the existence of many such protective deities, but the inclusion
of dates in inscriptions on them begins only around the eighteenth
century, making it no easy matter to set up a chronology of types ranging
all the way back to the earliest historic period. In any event, there is some
evidence for wayside protectors in phallic form in prehistoric times, at
which stage many may have been natural stones—as Shinto would
always prefer. The concept is directly related to fertility, as the use,
explicit nature of the sculptures and popular names often show. These
names also indicate their breadth of meaning: earth-ancestor deities,
road-ancestor deities, preventive deities, and holy sex deities.⁴ In other
words, they are rooted to the land, associated with the progenitors,
protectors against the evils of anything foreign, including 'foreigners'
from neighbouring villages, and associated with fertility. The word *sae*
is used interchangeably for holy and sex.

One type of dōsojin that may be seen along the roads are two figures
carved in high relief, one male, the other female, wearing long, heavy
costumes, standing frontally side by side in Siamese-twin proximity, or
pressed face to face. Most of the reliefs of recumbent figures shown in
sexual union were removed from the roadsides by the early twentieth
century, but several remain today as part of a considerable residue of
phallicism, despite official efforts a century ago to obliterate it. A traveller
needs to be more than a casual visitor to realize this.

In early centuries at least, these figures did not have any connection
with Buddhism, but with the passing of time the absorption of phallic
folk art into the repertory of Buddhist arts was neither resisted nor
considered to be abnormal. Sometimes referred to as Tantric arts, these

Plate 79

features are as much influenced by the folk arts as they are by Tantric ideas. One of the best known of these conversions is the popular little Jizō (Ksitigarbha) bodhisattva, which has tended to replace the dōsojin, often in groups of six, along the roads. With shaved head and simple cylindrical outline, he is intended to appear phallic, in particular from the back. A little less known to the public, the Dokoraku-jizō, Pleasure-loving Jizō, is associated with copulation.

The two National Museum figures are blended inseparably. The larger may hold a horn; the smaller holds the larger with an arm halfway round, but the left arm and shoulder melt into the back of the other. Typically heavy costumes do not simplify the problem of identification of details.

Plate 74

Back-to-back heads may be simpler versions of the dōsojin. The pair of heads on one slab in the grounds of the Tachibana-dera face roughly north and south, but the stone is now on the spot where the Lecture Hall once stood, west of the present Worship Hall, and therefore cannot be in its original place. It was probably moved two or three hundred years ago. The stone is more or less five-sided and the faces are more properly on its front corners. The north one is in higher relief and slightly greater detail; both have flattish, wide-proportioned, imbecilic expressions. The back of the stone is well smoothed. It has been suggested that it may have been attached to some structure.[5] The explanation furnished by the local priest is that the faces represent the duality of life, specifically, good and evil.[6]

Plates 75, 77

Four Saruishi (Monkey Stones) are now situated across the north-east side of a small circular tomb traditionally said to be that of a princess, a short walk from the Tachibana-dera station on the Kashiwara Line. They are known to have been moved at least twice. In 1702 they were extricated from rice fields and put on the south-west side of the large tomb attributed to Emperor Kimmei. The present location is only a short distance from Kimmei's tomb. The last removal may suggest some distaste for uncouth statuary associated with imperial tombs when the latter were being cleaned up as part of the revival of imperial power in the Meiji period, but the newfound aversion may have been tempered by an appreciation of their antiquity.

The two largest ones may be kneeling; the other two sitting. They are usually said to be two males and two females, but the details suggest otherwise. The largest is a nude male and appears to be humpbacked and paunched. Close inspection of the back gives the impression of a smaller figure merged with it, back-to-back. One female has a more obviously ape-like face, but all have rather similar inane and mindless expressions. One male figure is ithyphallic. The nudity of the figures is sufficient for a Japanese observer to regard these statues as animal and, indeed, historic Japanese art—erotic or otherwise—reflects the Japanese view that nudity was unattractive and abnormal for human beings. It is a satisfactory state for animals, which may then be anthropomorphized if human attributes or conditions are to be symbolized.

Plate 77

A rather odd passage in the *Kōko-nichi-roku* written in 1810 says that a long time ago four stone figures were dug out of a field near Emperor Kimmei's tomb by the local people and put on the tomb. One has four faces, two have three, and one has two. Their significance is unknown, but, it goes on to say, the workmen called them the Seven Happy Gods. Since the facts could have been checked at the time of writing and only one of these Monkey Stones conceivably fits the description, we are dealing with the loosest poetic licence or with other figures which are now lost. It is obvious, however, that the multifaced characteristic impressed the writer the most.

Tradition ascribes to these figures the same powers as deities of child-birth, but like the dōsojin, these were very likely once arranged by pairs and perhaps sat opposite each other along roads, as male and female wayside protectors were said to do originally, representing dualistic ideas that found no subtler means of expression.

One more of these stones, a male monkey, was moved to the Takatori Castle farther south in Nara prefecture when it was constructed in the seventeenth century. It apparently also came from the vicinity of Emperor Kimmei's tomb. More blocky than the others, little stone has been cut away except to shape the chest. The slightly wistful face is flattened and deeply outlined.

Plate 76

It has been said that there may be some relationship between these figures and remarks on burials for the 28th year of Empress Suiko's reign (620)[7] as recorded in the Nihon Shoki.[8] The reason for all of the activity there described is not explained, but it may have been the first time that graves were marked in a Buddhist fashion. Confusion not-withstanding, the story goes as follows: the crest of a tumulus was covered with stones. 'Outside the boundary the earth was piled up into a hill ...' and each *uji* (clan) was required to put up a large pillar on top of the hill. A man who outdid the others received the nickname, Great Pillar Atae.

It would be better in the translation to use the imperative since these were orders: cover the tomb with pebbles; pile up a hill; raise pillars; but perhaps this is immaterial. These 'pillars' (*hashira*) may be Buddhist epitaphs. However, any connection between Monkey Stones and pillars, posts or columns seems tenuous at best, and the author would not accept efforts to connect these stones with tomb cults.

There is only one other significant zoomorphic stone, so it hardly constitutes a class. It is an immense stone known as Kameishi, Turtle Stone, sitting in a field about 500 m. west of the Tachibana-dera. The slanted face looks towards the south-west. Features carved on the lower slope of this side resemble the upper part of a face, that is, an undulating line over closed eyelids. The sides have been worked in low relief and aid in producing the total effect of a dormant turtle. Perhaps the shape of the stone provided the initial inspiration, and then a minimum of carving produced the approximation of a turtle. A legend claimed to be 'old' might be passed on for its facetious value. When the neck of the turtle sticks out toward the west, the Yamato region will be transformed into a sea.[9] Old or otherwise, the Yamato region has little to fear from this somnolent creature.

A twelfth century record of the Kōfuku-ji names this stone as a boundary marker of the Yamato area, specifying its exact location. The stone seems not to have been moved, but few would accept any suggestion that it was first made as a boundary stone, or that the Yamato area was so precisely laid out when the stone is believed to have been carved.

It is said that there used to be a number of large stones in the Asuka region which were probably used for brewing rice-wine (*sake*) or pressing seeds for oil. Even if true, only one large one now remains. Popularly called Sakafune-ishi (Sake-boat-stone), it may be seen near the top of a low hill just above the Oka-dera, only a three minute walk from the one and only road running between the Ishibutai and the site of the Asuka-dera. Efforts were made to break it up when stones were being cut for the Takatori Castle, efforts that may have been more successful in other cases. Its two outer edges have been chipped off, but the total length of 5:45 m. is probably original, although the trough at the foot is broken.

Plate 82

Plate 84

The Sakafune-ishi rests in a level position and there is no particular reason to believe that it was not used exactly where it now lies. The circular and oval troughs vary between 7 and 11 cm. deep; the drains are shallower and are designed to permit lighter and more refined liquid to flow through, the heavier liquid and dregs to settle in the basins. The drains to the side basins would carry the thinnest liquid.

Similar stones may have been in use for at least a century and a half by this time. One small one, a stone replica with the drains and basin, was found in a fifth century tomb in the Tokyo area. In the history of sake brewing, more portable and manageable equipment was custom-arily used. The odds would certainly favour the making of oil, in all probability from sesame or rape seed. Sesame is known as far back as the Latest Jōmon period, or the first millenium BC, and may have been in common use by the Yayoi period in the production of oil.

Variations in the shapes of tombs were almost the rule during the awkward stage of transition from tumuli and hillside tunnel tombs to Buddhist ways of burial. The mound itself was sometimes dispensed with while sarcophagi and chambers were retained. One of the many articles in the Taika Reform regulated the mode of burial on the basis of rank, but failed to refer directly to sarcophagi. Instead, the regulations specified the 'inner dimensions' of the tomb. These were scaled by rank, as were the size and height of the mound, the number of workmen employed, and the number of days they could work. While the rather liberal allowance of 9 by 5 ft was good down to ministers of a lower class, all persons in ranks below that got a space only 9 by 4 ft and no mound to cover it. Human nature being what it is, a surmise here is that any unmounded but ingenious official could circumvent the law by figur-atively turning his tomb inside out and letting the sarcophagus impress the spectator. Since the dimensions of the internal spaces in two monu-ments, Masuda Iwafune and Oni no Setchin, come very close to what a ranked man was allowed who did not rate a mound, we may not be far off the mark in assuming that these gigantic hollowed out stones were sarcophagi, perhaps a consequence of their owners' loose interpretation of the law. In any case, Masuda Iwafune is more spectacular than most late tombs.

This Masuda Iwafune is an immense stone standing out in striking isolation on a hilltop well west of the Kume-dera. It is hewn out of a

Plate 80

153

natural rocky formation. Its surface is level on the north side and slanted on the south. Running more or less east and west is a depression with two deep and well-cut holes, though not precisely rectangular. The total length of the top part of the stone is about 7.5 m., and the way the upper part of this outcropping was cut down to the desired size may still be seen in the deep grooves on the lower exposed sides. In some places these grooves criss-cross each other, illustrating the coarse stoneworking methods of the Asuka period. The foot of the Turtle Stone is worked in the same way.

The Masuda Iwafune (Stone-boat) was believed by some to be the stone support for an epitaph written by Kōbō Daishi in 825 for the Masuda Pond, a pond ordered dug by Emperor Saga in 822. The pond has disappeared, the original epitaph has disappeared (though the inscription was copied), and most of the people who accepted the idea have disappeared.

While seeming a little unconventional, a double sarcophagus is not impossible. There is one in Fukuoka prefecture, for instance. These were especially for a husband and wife combination who, according to the old texts, were often buried together. The depression running the length of the surface may have taken lids, slid in from either side. The Iwayayama Tomb can be seen from here, the entrance to its stone corridor visible on the hillside, its interior exhibiting similarly fine workmanship. Such late sarcophagi in tomb chambers are usually hollowed out of one piece of stone.

If this is a double sarcophagus, each occupant would get almost the full inner length allowed all ranks, but a little less than the width allowed a man of the third rank (there were thirty ranks in all). He could have no mound, but to all intents and purposes he made up for it in the size of the sarcophagus.

There is more concensus on the humorously named Oni no Setchin (Devil's Toilet) and what may be its companion piece, Oni no Manaita (Devil's Chopping Board). These two objects lie on either side of a road in a spot called Kirigamine (Misty Summit), named from a popular legend that a devil caused the area to be covered by fog and then captured passers-by and used the flat stone to prepare them for eating.[10]

The large, hollowed out stone resting at an angle below the road is very likely the body of a sarcophagus which has slipped off the hill, while

Plates 81, 83

the slab lying flat above the road is probably its lid in an inverted position. As is the case with so many of these stones, drill and chisel marks show that an effort was made to break it up. By all standards, however, this would be a sarcophagus of phenomenal proportions. An open end has vertical recesses to take a door, but the dimensions of the lid are a little too large all round to fit well, which is the argument against the two being part and parcel of the same tomb. The cavity narrows slightly towards the bottom of the 'sarcophagus', but both its upper and lower lengths comfortably meet the 9 ft regulations for internal dimensions.

ASUKA NIIMASU SHRINE

A lesser known spot in the Asuka region (or at least foreign visitors are less frequently informed of its existence) is the Asuka Niimasu Shrine, located on a hill to the north-east of the Ango-in, the site of the Asuka-dera. Leading to decrepit buildings—which reflect the diffidence shown towards phallic cults today—are walkways lined with natural stones obviously chosen for their phallic shape. There may be as many as seventy in all. Larger ones are isolated on low terraces and marked off with straw ropes, the symbol of hallowed ground. The inner shrine, which is not visible to the public, has a platform supporting four stones each about one metre high.

Plate 85

The shrine has been called Moto-Ise (Original Ise), one of the many places where the Ise kami are supposed to have rested in their wanderings. The present form of the shrine is difficult to date, but it is mentioned in the tenth century *Engi-shiki* as a 'taisha,' a great shrine. The Shoku Nihongi says it was moved to this place in 829 from Kannabiyama, a hill not far away. The Nihon Shoki speaks of offerings being made to the 'four shrines of Asuka' in Temmu's reign, according to Aston's translation, but Asuka does not yet have four respectable shrines that would rate such attention, so one suspects a transcription error in an early text. Since the Engi-shiki often speaks of the 'four kami of Asuka,' it is most likely an idea of this sort that was intended. Three of these kami are male, one female.

The chief kami of Asuka Shrine is Kotoshironushi, son of the kami of the big Ōmiwa Shrine near Sakurai, a connection that puts Asuka Niimasu in a branch relationship. Kotoshironushi is not especially known as a phallic deity; in fact, his characteristics are not even well defined. Most likely an earlier phallic cult existed here, with which Kotoshironushi became later associated as the formalities of Shinto grew and the Ōmiwa Shrine took Asuka Niimasu under its wing. Asuka Niimasu is regarded as a 'male' shrine. Such shrines usually have 'female' counterparts not far away, in this case a shrine about five km. distant.

Asuka Niimasu Shrine has a big annual ceremony the equivalent of *taue*, the rice planting festival. It is claimed to be the only shrine to enact on stage a highly symbolic copulation ceremony between masked male and female figures using large straw objects. This performance may be only seven or eight hundred years old, according to the shrine's priest. The shrine, of course, has other, somewhat less spectacular ceremonies, and does a good wedding business today. It is also a mecca for married couples who have been childless for ten years or more.

In dealing with the dōsojin earlier, it was suggested that they were originally phallic stones. This section may be concluded, in defence of the inclusion of this shrine for this early date and this excursion into the local Shinto of Asuka, by saying that the shrine is a kind of archaeological anomaly, an island of original worship forms in a Buddhist sea, embodying the traditions that must have been commonplace at that time but are largely forgotten, or are supposed to be forgotten, today.

Connections with the stone work in Kyushu of the Tomb period are almost always raised as a possibility for the initial inspiration of the Asuka sculptures. While some connections cannot be ruled out entirely, the stones in Kyushu were designed specifically to stand on the mounds of tombs, the extant ones are chiefly of military figures, and they are usually more cubic in style. The connections could only be very remote at best.

On the other hand, some continental relationship should be considered. One automatically thinks of the various animals that form the independent stone sculptures of the Spirit Paths in the Han dynasty and later times in China. But stone figures were probably not associated with tombs in the Asuka region. Despite relatively little knowledge of early Korean stonework of this kind, the chances are best for inspiration of Korean origin, as is the case with so many cultural features at this stage of early Japanese history.

Conclusion

In supplementing conventional views of early Japanese history with such archaeological information as the remains of monuments in Asuka, interment and cremation practices, changes in temple architecture, the evolution of palaces, the nature of the defences, evidence for land dis~ tribution, the physical features of Heijō city, Shinto relics, coins in sites, and more, there is a tendency to judge the developments on the basis of geography, territory and terrain in regard to the consolidation of power centres. When imperial residences were constructed in the Asuka region in the late sixth and seventh centuries, tribal rivalries and political conditions limited most of the Korea~derived innovations to the confines of the court, which expended much of its energy in merely absorbing them. Rarely were efforts made to reach out beyond the Asuka region, except for the maintenance of the traditional communications with the port of Naniwa. The erection by Prince Shōtoku of one palace and at least three temples well outside Asuka were rare forays indeed by Plate 22 an unusual man; efforts that would have been out of character for a ruler himself and doubtless not much more typical for a prince charged with managing the affairs of state. It was not until the latter part of the seventh century and during the eighth century that the Ōtsu region along Lake Biwa was discovered as suitable for royal residence and the Yoshino mountains for retreats. Other areas were also explored.

The first major outward sign of power consolidation was the establish~ ment of the capital at Fujiwara in 694. Its founding was based on the realization that centralized controls could not be achieved without geographic stability. The Chinese~style, formal capital city had the physical shape and the political organization to bolster the emperor's position at the apex of the social pyramid, and it brought together within a fixed area other groups of people, notably the monks, who, in this case, added an extra dimension to the social structure not unlike another powerful family.

By the time the capital was moved to Heijō in 710, the machinery was in working order, in the form of the Taihō Civil and Penal Codes, for the emperor to exercise full authority on a national scale. The official arts were diffused from court workshops through provincial headquarters and cloisters, and as the bureaucracy promoted local craftsmanship and provincial materials, especially in textiles, the arts expanded greatly in variety. Outside the court, the chief function of art was to serve the needs of the temples but it also served society as a whole through a wide range of materials and techniques in religious, court and domestic architecture, sculpture, painting, metalwork, lacquer, pottery and textiles. Reflecting the preoccupation of society with rank, the arts tended to be graded for consumption by social classes; the minor arts that were regarded as the most peculiarly Chinese in style outranked the others.

The court art of Shōmu was competing in the international field, and his architectural projects were intended to meet international standards. Thanks to the efficiency of the Nara legal system, the Provincial Temples were built as ordered, as archaeology has been able to show where investigation has been possible. The accoutrements of Buddhism nourished aristocratic vanities; the temples became prestige symbols while they acted as welfare agencies and literary centres. Shinto played the opposite role; its less obtrusive beliefs and ceremonies had both a levelling and unifying effect on the social strata and were a common meeting ground for larger communities.

The cultural plateau reached in the eighth century was in direct consequence of the strengthened imperial position, supported by the Chinese-inspired legal system of the time. The peak of imperial power was never again eclipsed; the scale of the Tōdai-ji, Saidai-ji, Shin-yakushi-ji and Daian-ji was rarely again surpassed. But, after the transfer of the capital to Heian in 794, the emperors lost much of their power to the heads of the leading families, establishing a pattern of relationship that lasted until the capital was moved to Edo (Tokyo) in 1868–9.

Notes on the Text

ABBREVIATIONS

NKGJ *Nihon Kōkogaku Jiten*
(Dictionary of Japanese Archaeology): see
Fujita
NKIK *Nihon Kodai Iseki no Kenkyū*
(Study on Ancient Japanese Sites): see
Saitō
NKZM *Nihon Kōkogaku Zuroku Mokuroku*
(Illustrated Catalogue of Japanese Archae-
ology): see Saitō
SKGT *Sekai Kōkogaku Taikei*
(Series of World Archaeology): see Asano
and Kobayashi

CHAPTER II

1 See T. Satō, *Some problems of the Wadō-
kaichin*, p. 364 (English summary) for the
arguments about both the reading and the
writing of the characters. The second and
fourth may be simplifications, but the latter
may not be a simplification of 'treasure', the
character which appears on all other Japanese coins, but rather of 'precious'; hence
chin and not *hō* is the preferred Japanese
pronunciation.
2 Y. Kobayashi in *SKGT*, p. 7.
3 N. Kōga, *Analysis list of old coins*, p. 432.
4 Y. Kobayashi in *SKGT*, p. 8.
5 Satō, *Some problems of the Wadō-kaichin*, p.
332.
6 In Nara city: Kasuga shrine, Kōfuku-ji
grounds, under the platform in the Kōfuku-
ji Main Hall, Gankō-ji pagoda, Shinyaku-
shi-ji, Hokke-ji, Yokoi-hai-ji; Yakushi-ji

Main Hall, Yakushi-ji west pagoda, Saidai-
ji grounds, Saidai-ji east pagoda; in Nara
prefecture: Daruma-dera at Ōji-chō, Kita-
katsuragi county; Taima-dera grounds at
Taima village, Kita-katsuragi county;
Taima-dera west pagoda; Nyoirin-ji at
Yoshino-chō, Yoshino county; in Kyoto
city: Kamigamo shrine; in Kyoto prefecture:
Kaishō-ji grounds in Tsuzuki county,
Tanabe-chō; in Shiga prefecture: Sūfuku-ji
in Ōtsu city; in Gifu prefecture: South Great
Gate, Provincial Temple in Akasaka-chō,
Fuwa county.
7 Satō, *Some problems of the Wadō-kaichin*, p.
324.
8 R. K. Reischauer, *Early Japanese History*,
Part A, p. 192.

CHAPTER III

1 K. Harada in Society for the Restoration of
Munakata Jinja, *Okinoshima*, II, p. 285.
2 The Nippon Gakujutsu Shinkōkai, *The
Manyōshū*, p. 256.
3 S. Narasaki, *Sanage kilns*, pp. 3, 26.
4 *Ibid.*, p. 16.

CHAPTER IV

1 *NKGJ*, p. 262.
2 Y. Tamura, *Reflections on the Asuka and
Fujiwara Capitals*, pp. 34–35.
3 Kudō in *SKGT*, p. 18
4 *NKGJ*, p. 162.
5 Kudō in *SKGT*, p. 26.

6 *Kōkogaku Journal* 40/1, p. 22 (Notes on illustrations).

7 T. Saitō, *NKIK*, p. 293.

8 *Ibid.*, p. 295.

9 *Ibid.*, p. 289.

10 *Ibid.*

11 *Ibid.*, p. 276.

CHAPTER V

1 Kudō in *SKGT*, p. 17.

2 *NKGJ*, pp. 332–333.

3 K. Tsuboi in *SKGT*, p. 63.

4 S. Kuwahara, *Taga-jō abandoned temple*, pp. 19–20.

5 Tsuboi in *SKGT*, p. 66.

6 *Ibid.*, p. 68.

7 *NKGJ*, p. 5.

8 W. G. Aston, *Nihongi*, I, p. 203.

9 T. Saitō, *NKZM*, p. 159.

CHAPTER VI

1 J. Sawamura in *SKGT*, p. 56.

2 Aston, *Nihongi*, II, p. 249: termed a shingle-roof.

3 Aston romanizes it as 'Kahara.' As he says in note 5, p. 249: 'This name is written with characters which mean river-bed . . . but also means tiles, which in this connection does not seem a mere fortuitous coincidence.' Kawahara is literally 'river-field' and may be contracted in the spoken language as 'kawara,' but it was, in fact, not an exploited coincidence: there is nothing to indicate that the Kawahara Palace had any tiled roofs.

4 *Ibid.*, p. 320; probably actually more west than south.

5 Tamura, *Reflections*, p. 33–34; Y. Kudō, *Fujiwara Palace*, p. 36.

6 Kudō, *Fujiwara Palace*, p. 34.

7 Kudō in *SKGT*, p. 22.

8 Kudō, *Fujiwara Palace*, p. 35.

9 *Ibid.*, p. 27.

10 S. Kojima, *The Archaeology of Nara Prefecture*, p. 279.

11 T. Kishi in K. Tsuboi and T. Kishi, *Ancient Japan*, pp. 248ff.

12 *Ibid.*, p. 256.

13 Kamei, *Heijō Palace*, p. 191.

14 K. Kitō, *Wooden tallies unearthed at Heijō Palace in 1966*, p. 31: 18,366 of these wooden tallies were recorded as of 1966.

15 See T. Yamane, *Naniwa Palace*, list following p. 267 for a full chronology of developments connected with the Naniwa palaces.

16 Kudō in *SKGT*, p. 25.

17 Aston, *Nihongi*, II, p. 380; for instance, Emperor Temmu died in the 'principal' palace.

18 Reischauer, *Early Japanese History*, Part A, pp. 216–217, gives all possible reasons for the removal from Heijō.

19 T. Katsuno, *Religious policy in the reign of Emperor Kammu*, p. 354 (English summary).

CHAPTER VII

1 Saitō, *NKZM*, p. 141.

2 *Ibid.*, p. 136.

3 M. Ishida, *On the central foundation stones of pagodas*, II, pp. 159, 161.

4 Aston, *Nihongi*, II, p. 67.

5 The texts mention these: Kōgen-ji, built in 553 by Soga Iname, once called the Toyura-dera, at Toyura, Asuka village, Takechi county, Nara prefecture; Yoshino-dera, first mentioned in 554; and Daibetsuō-ji, first mentioned in 577. The word 'temple' was undoubtedly loosely used in connection with these places of worship.

6 Aston, *Nihongi*, II, p. 101.

7 K. Asano in *SKGT*, p. 32.

8 *Ibid.*, pp. 33–34.

9 S. Mizuno, *Hōryū-ji*, pp. 23–25, places the Yakushi later than the Shaka on stylistic grounds; see A. Soper, *Notes on Hōryū-ji and the Sculpture of the 'Suikō Period'*, pp. 91–93 for a summary of the problems.

10 K. Machida, *A Historical Survey of the Controversy as to Whether the Hōryū-ji was rebuilt or not*, p. 89.

11 R. Paine and A. Soper, *The Art and Architecture of Japan*, p. 176 and elsewhere.

12 Asano in *SKGT*, p. 35.

13 J. Murata and T. Ueno, *Hōryū-ji*, p. 37; M. Ōoka, *Temples of Nara*, inserted chart before p. 69.

14 S. Tanaka, *Study of the Wall Paintings of Japan*, pp. 21–23, thinks they should have been done in the Tempyō-shōhō era (749–757) after a large 749 imperial donation to private temples.

15 Mizuno, *Hōryū-ji*, p. 118.

16 *NKGJ*, p. 500.

17 M. Ishida, *Study of the Sites of Temples of the Asuka Period*, pp. 87–93; later research has modified the statistics, but has not changed the fundamental evidence for the developments.

18 Tamura, *Reflections*, p. 27.

19 M. Ōoka, J. Murata, T. Fukuyama and K. Asano, *Excavation of the South Great Gate and Middle Gate of Yakushi-ji*, p. 149.

20 K. Machida (chief author), *Yakushi-ji*, p. 40.

21 Ōoka *et al.; op. cit.*, p. 147.

22 See T. Kuno and T. Inoue, *Study of the Yakushi Triad in the Kondō Yakushi-ji*, for an extensive discussion of the arguments.

23 *Ibid.*, p. 106.

24 Aston, *Nihongi*, II, pp. 357ff always trans-lates the name of this particular temple, but normally not others: the Great Temple in the Great Palace.

25 Asano in *SKGT*, p. 36.

26 *Ibid.*, p. 38.

27 *Ibid.*

28 *Ibid.*, p. 39.

29 M. Ishida, *Tōdai-ji and Provincial Temples*,

30 Saeki, *A Study of Shinsen Shōjiroku*, pp. 296–297.

CHAPTER VIII

1 S. Umehara, *Essays on Japanese Archaeology*, p. 80.

2 T. Saitō, *Several thoughts on Shōgakusan burial mounds*, pp. 154–155.

3 Saitō, *NKIK*, p. 349.

4 See Society for the Study of Historical Periods, *Problems*.

5 I. Hori, *Japanese Religion*, p. 224.

6 *Ibid.*, pp. 223 ff.

7 The Nippon Gakujutsu Shinkōkai, *Manyōshū*, pp. 51, 186.

8 S. Mizuno and Y. Kobayashi, *Illustrated Dictionary of Archaeology*, p. 237.

9 *Ibid.*

10 *NKGJ*, p. 156.

11 S. Mizuno in *SKGT*, p. 106.

CHAPTER IX

1 K. Tsuboi in *SKGT*, p. 98.

2 Aston, *Nihongi*, II, p. 251.

3 Tsuboi in *SKGT*, p. 98, quoting Ishida and Yajima.

4 D. Richie and K. Ito, *The Erotic Gods*, p. 52.

5 Tsuboi in *SKGT*, p. 97.

6 Iwanami, *Asuka*, p. 25.

7 Tsuboi in *SKGT*, p. 97.

8 Aston, *Nihongi*, II, pp. 147–148.

9 Iwanami, *Asuka*, p. 6.

10 *Ibid.*, p. 5.

Bibliography

The Japanese bibliography is written entirely in English, transliteration having been omitted at the request of the publisher in order to conserve space. The reader will find summaries in English where the work quoted is marked with an asterisk.

Books and Articles in Japanese

AOYAMA, S., *The Period of the Heijō Capital*, Tokyo 1965.

ASAHI NEWSPAPER PUBLISHERS, *History of Money*, Tokyo 1957.

—*Heijō Palace Exhibition; Excavated Capital of the Nara Period*, Tokyo 1969.

ASANO, K., and KOBAYASHI, Y., editors, *SKGT*, 4 (Japan IV), Tokyo 1964.

COMMISSION FOR THE PROTECTION OF CULTURAL PROPERTIES, COMMEMORAT-IVE VOLUME, *Hōryū-ji Wakakusa-garan Site: Preliminary Report on the Excavation of 1969*, Tokyo 1970.

*EGAMI, N., SEKINO, T. and SAKURAI, K., *Tate Sites: A Study of Settlement Sites in the North Eastern Region of Japan*, Tokyo 1958.

FUJISHIMA, G., chief author, *Shitennō-ji*, Tokyo 1967.

FUJITA, R., editor, *Dictionary of Japanese Archaeology*, Tokyo 1962.

FUKUYAMA, T., *Temples of Japan: Nara*, Tokyo 1961

—*Temples of Japan: Kyoto*, Tokyo 1961.

FUKUYAMA, T., chief author, *Excavation of Nagaoka Capital*, Tokyo 1968.

FUKUYAMA, T. and KUNO, T., *Yakushi-ji*, Tokyo, 2nd ed. 1963.

HACHIŌJI CITY, FUNADA SITE INVESTI-GATION COMMITTEE, *Funada, Archaeology Journal*, 40, 1970.

HIGO, K., *Study of the Site of the Ōtsu Capital*, Ōtsu 1940.

HORI, I., *Japanese Religion*, Tokyo, 11th ed. 1966.

ISHIDA, M., *Study of the Excavation of Buddhist Remains of Nachi Sūtra Mounds*, Tokyo 1927.

—On the central foundation stones of pagodas, *Journal of Archaeology* XXII/2, 1932, pp. 77–91; XXII/3, 1932, pp. 148–169.

—*Study of the Sites of Temples of the Asuka Period*, Tokyo 1944.

—*Tōdai-ji and Provincial Temples*, Tokyo 1959.

—*Underground Treasures of the Tempyō Period*, Tokyo 1961.

—*Hōryū-ji Memoranda*, Tokyo 1969.

—*Hōryū-ji* (in series *Hihō: Secret Treasures*), Tokyo 1970.

IUCHI, K., The development of early temple plans, *Historic Sites and Art*, XXXV/10, 1965, pp. 384–401.

IWANAMI PHOTOGRAPHIC LIBRARY, *Asuka* (130), Tokyo 1954.

JAPANESE HISTORICAL ARCHAEOLOGY SOCIETY, *Collection of Studies on Japanese Historical Archaeology*, Tokyo 1966 (30 articles, chiefly on Buddhist archaeology).

KAMEI, K., editor, *Heijō Palace*, Tokyo 1963.

KASHIWARA ARCHAEOLOGICAL INSTITUTE, *Collected Articles on the Ancient Culture of Kinki*, Tokyo 1963.

*KATSUNO, T., The religious policy under the reign of Emperor Kammu, *Palaeologia*, X/2–4, 1962, pp. 330–342.

KAWASAKI, T., The end of the Tomb period and the spread of cremation tombs to remote places, *Yamagata Historical Studies*, 5, 1967, pp. 99–168.

KIDA, T., *Imperial Capitals*, Tokyo 1915.

KINOSHITA, R., On the relationship between Provincial Headquarters and the *jōri* system,

Historical Studies, L/5, 1966, pp. 73–102.

KITŌ, K., Wooden tallies unearthed at Heijō Palace in 1966, *Annual Report for 1967 of the National Commission for the Protection of Cultural Properties of Nara Prefecture*, pp. 31–34.

KODAMA K., editor, *Cultural History of Japan Series*, III, Nara Period, Tokyo 1956.

KŌGA, N., Analysis list of old coins, *Journal of Archaeology*, IX/7, 1919, pp. 415–432.

KOJIMA, S., *The Archaeology of Nara Prefecture*, Tokyo 1965.

KUDŌ, Y., *Fujiwara Palace*, Tokyo 1967.

KURATA, O., Studies in sūtra mounds; articles in *Museum*, 1963: 147, 148, 152; 1964: 154, 156, 159; 1965: 174, 176, 177; 1966: 178, 179, 181, 183, 184.

KUWAHARA, S., Taga-jō abandoned temple, *Archaeology Journal*, 11/8, 1967, pp. 16–20.

KYOTO PREFECTURE EDUCATION COM-MITTEE, *The Site of Nagaoka Palace*, Kyoto 1966.

MACHIDA, K., *Yakushi-ji*, Tokyo 1960.

—*Hōryū-ji*, Tokyo 1967.

MIZUNO, S., *Hōryū-ji*, Tokyo 1965.

MIZUNO, S. and KOBAYASHI, Y., *Illustrated Dictionary of Archaeology*, Tokyo 1959.

MORI, O., Summary of the survey of the Zutō Buddhist mound, *Annual Report for 1961 of the National Commission for the Protection of Cultural Properties of Nara Prefecture*.

*MURATA, J. and UENO, T., *Hōryū-ji*, Tokyo, Osaka, Moji and Nagoya 1960.

NARASAKI, S., *Sanage Kilns*, Tokyo 1966.

NARASAKI, S. and MIKAMI T., *Historical Periods*, 1 and 2, (*The Archaeology of Japan*, vols VI and VII), Tokyo 1967.

NANIWA PALACE SITE INVESTIGATION COM-MITTEE, *Studies on the Site of Naniwa Palace*, vols I-IV, Osaka 1956–61.

NARA PREFECTURE EDUCATION COM-MITTEE, *The Site of Fujiwara Palace: A Brief Report of the Excavation of 1966*, Nara 1967.

NARA PREFECTURE NATIONAL COMMISSION FOR THE PROTECTION OF CULTURAL PROPERTIES, *Report on the Excavation of the Asuka-dera*, Nara 1958.

—*Report on the Excavation of Heijō Palace*, II, Tenri, 1962; III, Tenri, 1963; IV, Nara 1966.

—*A Brief Report of the Excavation of the Heijō Palace Site in 1964*, Nara 1965.

—*Short Report on the Excavation of Heijō Palace in 1965*, Nara 1966.

—*Short report on the Excavation of Heijō Palace in 1966*, Nara 1967.

OBATA, A., *Coinage of Japan*, Tokyo 1966.

—*A History of Mines*, Tokyo 1966.

OCHIAI, S., *The Jōri System*, Tokyo 1967.

ŌMI ANCIENT ARTS TAIKAN PUBLISHING SOCIETY, *The Site of the Ōtsu Capital: Its Related Sites and their Finds*, Kyoto 1960.

ŌOKA, M., *Temples of Nara*, Tokyo 1965.

ŌOKA, M., MURATA, J., FUKUYAMA, T. and ASANO, K., Excavation of the South Great Gate and Middle Gate of Yakushi-ji, *Papers of the Society of Japanese Architecture*, 49, 1955, pp. 142–149.

SAEKI, A., *A Study of 'Shinsen Shōjiroku'*, Tokyo 1963.

SAITŌ, T., *Illustrated Japanese Archaeology*, Tokyo 1955.

—*Studies on Ancient Japanese Sites*, Tokyo 1968.

*—Several thoughts on Shōgakusan burial mounds, *Palaeologia*, XVI/2-4, 1969, pp. 145–155.

*SATŌ, T., Some problems of the Wadō-kaichin, *Palaeologia*, XI, 1964, pp. 321–333.

Early Buddhist Japan

SHIBATA, M., *The Site of the Ōtsu Capital: The Sūfuku-ji Site*, Ōtsu city 1941.

*SOCIETY FOR THE RESTORATION OF MUNAKATA JINJA, *Okinoshima*, Tokyo, vol. I, 1959; vol. II, 1961.

SOCIETY FOR THE STUDY OF HISTORICAL PERIODS, Problems concerning cremation tombs, *Wakagi Kōko*, 84, 1967, pp. 4–6.

SUMITA, S. and NAITŌ, M., *Old Tiles*, Tokyo 1968.

TAMURA, Y., *Reflections on the Asuka and Fujiwara Capitals*, Kyoto, 4th edition, 1968.

—*Yakushi-ji*, Osaka 1965.

TANAKA, S., *Study of the Wall Paintings of Japan*, Osaka 1944.

—Old literature concerning Prince Shōtoku's Shinaga tomb, *Journal of Archaeology*, XXXIV/9, 1944, pp. 496–519.

*TOKYO NATIONAL MUSEUM, *Illustrated Catalogue of Tokyo National Museum Objects Excavated from Sūtra Mounds*, Tokyo 1967.

—*Japanese Archaeology Exhibition*, Tokyo 1969. (English list of plates)

—*Report on the Excavation of the Tō-in of Hōryū-ji*, Tokyo 1948.

TSUBOI, K. and KISHI, T., editors, *Ancient Japan 5: Kinki Region*, Tokyo 1970.

TSUNODA, B., *Study of Provincial Temples*, 2 vols, Kyoto 1938.

UENO, G. and TATSUMI, S., *Study of the Sūtra Mounds of Shingū, Kumano*, Shingū 1963.

UMEHARA, S., *Essays on Japanese Archaeology*, Tokyo 1940.

YAMANE, T., *Naniwa Palace*, Tokyo 1964.

Books and Articles in English

ASTON, W. G., (translator) *Nihongi*, 2 vols, London 1896.

HALL, J. W., *Japan: From Prehistory to Modern Times*, New York 1970.

KAMSTRA, J. H., *Encounter or Syncretism: The Initial Growth of Japanese Buddhism*, Leiden 1967.

KIDDER, J. E., *Japanese Temples*, Tokyo and Amsterdam 1964.

KUNO, T. and INOUE, T., Study of the Yakushi Triad in the Kondō Yakushi-ji, *Acta Asiatica* I, 1960, pp. 89–108.

MACHIDA, K., A Historical Survey of the Controversy as to Whether the Hōryū-ji was rebuilt or not, *Acta Asiatica* 15, 1968, pp. 87–115.

NAITŌ, T., (translated and edited by W. R. B. Acker and B. Rowland), *The Wall-Paintings of Hōryūji*, Baltimore 1943.

NIPPON GAKUJUTSU SHINKŌKAI (translator), *Manyōshū*, New York, 1969.

PAINE, R. and SOPER, A. C., *The Art and Architecture of Japan*, Baltimore 1969.

PONSONBY-FANE, R. A. B., Ancient Capitals and Palaces of Japan, *Transactions of the Japan Society of London*, XX, 1923.

REISCHAUER, R. K., *Early Japanese History*, 2 vols, Princeton 1937.

RICHIE, D. and ITO, K., *The Erotic Gods: Phallicism in Japan*, Tokyo 1967.

SANSOM, G., *A History of Japan to 1334*, Stanford 1958.

SAUNDERS, E. D., *Buddhism in Japan*, Philadelphia 1964.

SOPER, A. C., *The Evolution of Buddhist Architecture in Japan*, Princeton 1942.

—Notes on Hōryūji and the Sculpture of the 'Suikō Period', *Art Bulletin*, XXXIII, 1951, pp. 77–94.

VISSER, M. W. DE, *Ancient Buddhism in Japan*, 2 vols, Tokyo 1935.

1

2

3

4

5

6

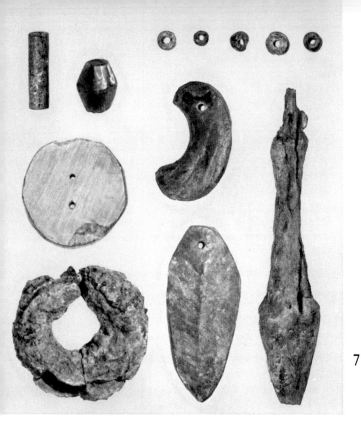

7

8

9

10

11

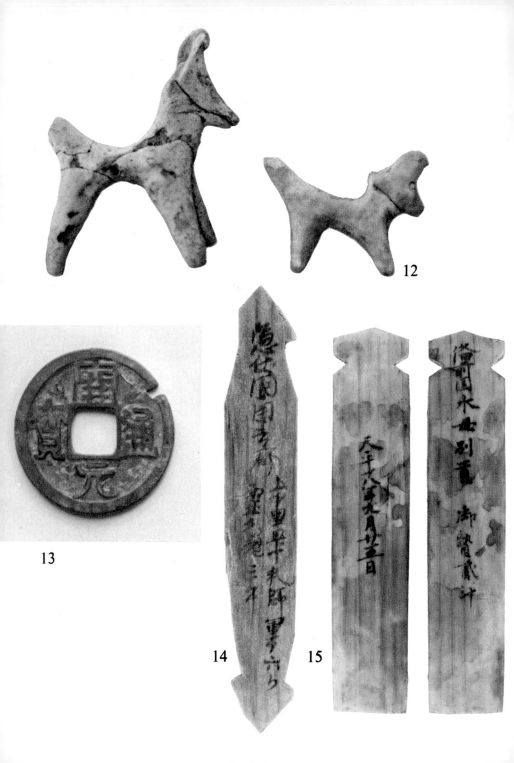

12

13

14   15

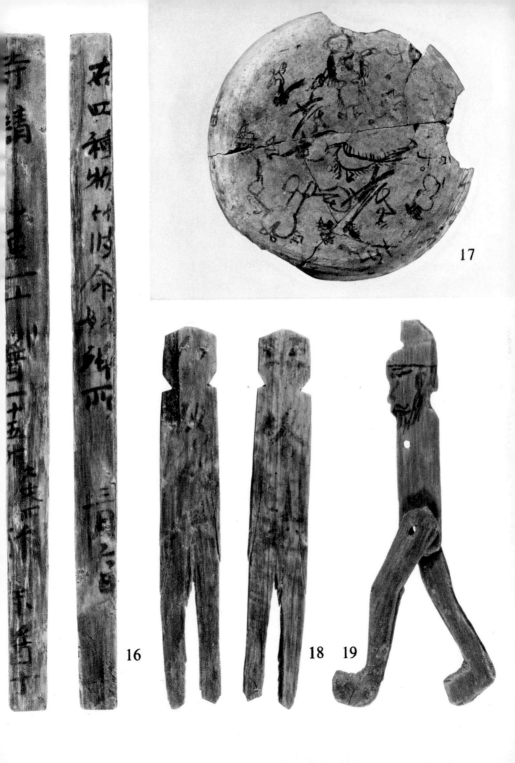

16

17

18 19

20

21

22

23

24

25

26

27

28

29

30

31

32   33   34

35

36

37

38

39

40

41

42

43

44

45

46

47

48

49

52

53

54

55

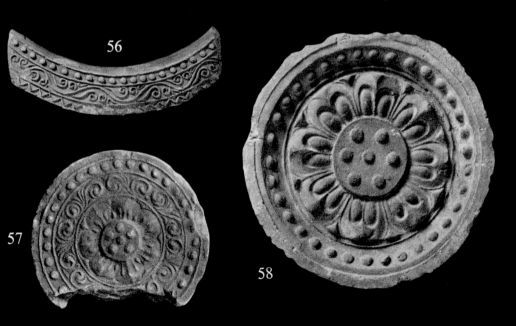

56

57

58

59

60

61

62

63

64

65

66

67, 68

69

70

71

72

73

74,75

76,77

78,79

80

81

82

83

84

85

86

87

88

Sources of Illustrations

PLATES Mr. Hiroshi Kitazawa, 3; Nachi Shrine Office, 8; Fukuoka Prefectural Office, 10; Mr. Taku Tanaka and the Nara Cultural Properties Committee, 11, 14–19, 21; Nagano Rokumeisō, 24, 26, 30, 31, 42–48, 73, 86–88; Asuka-en, 36; National Museum, Tokyo, 53, 56–58, 66–68, 70; Mr. Kōichi Shirakawa, 54. Plate 69 from *The Site of the Ōtsu Capital*, pl. 2.

FIGURES Many of the figures have been redrawn or otherwise modified for this book. Except for 24, 32, 52 and 56, which are too composite to include, the figures are derived as follows, listed respectively: Figs 8, 50 from Kodama, *Cultural History of Japan* Series III, figs 142, 83; Figs 9, 11, 12, 13, 14, 15, 17, 23, 27, 34, 36, 43, 51, 55, 66 from Asano and Kobayashi, *SKGT* IV, figs 24, 44, 106, 108, 115, 119 and 120, 97, 56, 48, 60 and 66, 63 and 65, 78 and 68, 79, 73 and 82, 200; Figs 10, 42, 48 from Fujita, *NKGJ*, pp. 162, 500, 320; Figs 16, 20 from *Heijō Palace Exhibition*; Fig. 19 from Fukuyama, *Excavation of Naga-oka Capital*, p. 144; Fig. 22 from Kamei, *Heijō Palace*, fig. 14; Fig. 40 from Mizuno, *Hōryū-ji*, fig. 96; Figs 46, 53 from Ōoka, *Temples of Nara*, fig. 45; Fig. 57 from Ume-hara, *Essays on Japanese Archaeology*, pp. 77, 81; Fig. 61 from Ishida, *Hōryū-ji Memoranda*, pp. 272, 273; Fig. 63 from Ueno and Tatsumi, *Study of the Sūtra Mounds of Shingū, Kumano*, fig. 13; Fig. 67 from Mori, *Summary of the Survey of the Zutō Buddhist Mound*.

Notes on the Plates

1 Reconstructed pit-dwelling, Hiraide, Soga village, Higashi-chikuma county, Nagano prefecture. Square pit with rounded corners 6.3 by 6 m. Middle to Late Tomb period (fifth to sixth centuries). The house has four main pillars with a clay oven against the middle of the east wall and large storage pits to either side. The original house on this site had been destroyed by fire and its floor had been rebuilt.

2 Typical pit-dwelling of the Funada site, Nagafusa-chō, Hachiōji city, (greater) Tokyo. Average size about 6.3 by 5.5 m. Late Tomb period (sixth century).

3 Aerial view of a part of sections C and D of the excavations of the Funada site, Nagafusa-chō, Hachiōji city, (greater) Tokyo. Approximately 100 pit-dwellings may be seen in this view of the vast Funada residential site. Section C had one Middle Jōmon period dwelling, 47 of the Late Tomb period, 13 of historic periods, and 40 others; section D had 4 of the Yayoi period, 65 of the Late Tomb period, 24 of historic periods and one other. Photograph taken early in 1969.

4 Kagenoma stone defences, Kaita village, Kaho county, Fukuoka prefecture. Probably seventh century. A long line of stones averaging about one metre in height running along the side of a hill marks part of the outlines of this fortification. Located above the right bank of the Onga River, the average elevation is 80 m. One theory claims that such stones were simply supports for high earthen walls that formed a protective ring around the top of the hill.

5 Wall with a water sluice: part of the Goshogatani stone defences, Kyōbashi city (jurisdictional area), Fukuoka prefecture. The height of the wall is about 10 m. Probably seventh century. Goshogatani has about 3 km. of walls, situated at an altitude of 247 m. There are several 'water gates'.

6 View from Misaka Pass (immediate foreground) looking toward Shinano (Nagano prefecture). Travellers had to negotiate the rugged terrain to reach the Kantō region, and left offerings here to the kami, forming a large accumulation of Shinto ritual objects ranging in date from the fifth to the fifteenth centuries. The main arteries were changed in later times. The sharp V-shape in the second range is Amikake Pass, and the distant skyline is the Akashi mountains.

7 Shinto ritual objects from Misaka Pass, Achi village, Shimo-ina county, Nagano prefecture. Prehistoric to seventh century. Numerous objects and stone replicas have been found here. *Below left*, copies of bronze mirrors and swords are made of a bluish schist, perforated for tying to trees. *Above left*, tubular and hexagonal beads are of glass, other beads of stone, and the arrow-head, *right*, of iron. Stone replicas were replaced at Misaka by offerings of paper, cloth or wood after the middle of the seventh century. All actual size.

8 Bronze statuette of Kannon, from the Shinto ritual site at Nachi, Katsuura-chō, Wakayama prefecture. Height 39.7 cm. Eighth century. National Museum, Tokyo. Several small bronze Buddhist figures were found at Nachi, not far from the waterfalls. Such a

figure must be dated stylistically, the chief criteria being the fullness of the face, the forward curve of the body and the rather thin drapery.

9 A section of the remains of the Asuka Itabuki Palace, Asuka village, Takechi (or Takaichi) county, Nara prefecture. Probably mid-seventh century. The well measures about 10 × 10 m., and is 8 m. deep. This may have been where the wine was made, if the facilities at Heijō Palace can be taken as a guide to Itabuki.

10 Excavation of South Gate and Middle Gate (foreground) of Dazaifu, Dazaifu-chō, Tsukushi county, Fukuoka prefecture. Seventh to eighth centuries. These 1968–70 excavations revealed that there were two south gates on the spot and four or more middle gates. A moat lay to the south of the South Gate. The site was a village of the Middle Tomb period (fifth century) marked by post-holes, the presence of which also showed that the earlier middle gates lacked stone bases. Eventually small stones were used for a Middle Gate and, later, large slabs were placed over these. At the top left, for instance, can be seen a large stone base for a wooden column resting on smaller stones.

11 Wood frame well, south-east sector of Heijō Palace, Saki-chō, Nara city (jurisdictional area). Outer frame about 2.7 by 2.6 m. Eighth century. Several wells have been uncovered at Heijō Palace, and their contents often appear to reveal current cult practices, the good condition of many objects indicating ritual deposits. This one contained many pottery vessels and wooden utensils. Wells have yielded wooden tallies, wooden dolls, coins and other objects.

12 Two clay horses, Heijō Palace, Saki-chō,

Nara city (jurisdictional area). Height of smaller horse 7.3 cm. Eighth century. These are reddish Haji ware, the traditional material for domestic, low-fired pottery.

13 Kaitsū-genhō (Chinese: K'ai-tung-yüan-pao) copper coin found on the International Christian University site, Mitaka, (greater) Tokyo. Diameter 2.4 cm. First minted in 621 by Emperor Kao-tsung, these coins were issued intermittently in China with little change for about three centuries. Thousands were brought to Japan and some examples have been found in sūtra mounds of the Late Heian (894–1185) and Kamakura (1185–1333) periods.

14 Inscribed wooden tally, Heijō Palace, Saki-chō, Nara city (jurisdictional area). Length 17 cm. 716–17. Tallies record taxes, gifts and various other transactions of goods at the palace. This tally carries an inscription on one side only, two small sections of which are not legible: '*Oki-kuni Suki-gun . . . sato . . . wakame rokuretsu. Reiki 3.*' In other words, the tax came from an individual or a family whose address is a land allocation unit in Suki county of Oki province (islands now belonging to Shimane prefecture); he or they sent six strands of seaweed in the year 716–717.

15 Inscribed wooden tally, Heijō Palace, Saki-chō, Nara city (jurisdictional area). Length 14.4 cm. 746. The inscription on two sides reads as follows: 'Bizen-kuni *kurage* special donation. For the emperor's honourable diet, two *to*. Tempyō 18, 9th month, 25th day.' Kurage is probably jelly fish. Therefore, Emperor Shōmu received a special gift of about 8 gallons of jelly fish from Bizen province on the 25th day of September, 746.

16 Inscribed wooden tally, Heijō Palace, Saki-

chō, Nara city (jurisdictional area). Length 25.9 cm.; width 1.9 cm.; thickness 0.4 cm. Probably 763 or 764. According to the inscription on both sides of this *hinoki* (Japanese cypress) tally, a temple wanted about 4 gallons of red beans, about 6 gallons of soya sauce, some vinegar and fermented soybean paste. Three small letters on the front side show that the goods were intended for the kitchen of the temple in which the empress had retired.

17 Pottery plate with black ink sketches, Heijō Palace, Saki-chō, Nara city (jurisdictional area). Diameter 19.9 cm. Eighth century. The meaning of the sketches is not clear.

18 Inscribed wooden figure, Heijō Palace, Saki-chō, Nara city (jurisdictional area). Height 15 cm. Eighth century. A flat wooden voodoo figure with illegible inscription on both sides was found in another well in the same sector as that shown in Plate 11. This moustached and presumably male figure has had small wooden pegs driven through each eye and a longer one through the heart. Apparently used in magical practices against a rival, it is graphic testimony to a handful of references in the traditional literature of this date in which women performed the ceremonies intended to eliminate an unwanted person, usually a relative.

19 Wooden puppet figure with moveable arms and legs, Heijō Palace, Saki-chō, Nara city (jurisdictional area). Length 14.7 cm. Eighth century. There was already a varied fare of dramatic performances by the eighth century, and puppetry is thought to have already been in vogue, perhaps not only at the court.

20 Preserved area of the Imperial Council Hall of Nagaoka Palace, Mukō-machi, Otokuni county, Kyoto prefecture. 784–794. Located south-west of Kyoto (Heian), the remains of the capital of Nagaoka are known through several excavations of parts of the palace.

21 Aerial view of excavation of extreme northern part of the Imperial Residence, believed to be the kitchen, Heijō Palace, Saki-chō, Nara city (jurisdictional area). Eighth century.

22 Shitennō-ji, Moto-machi, Tennōji ward, Osaka city. Original temple 593; rebuilt 1958. Destroyed during an air raid on Osaka during World War II, this temple has been reconstructed in reinforced concrete, with all due regard to stylistic accuracy. It is not only the type temple for the so-called Kudara Style but the only one remaining of at least a dozen known to have been built in the late sixth and early seventh centuries.

23 Site of West Main Hall (foreground) and pagoda (midground), Kawahara-dera, Kawahara, Asuka village, Takechi county, Nara prefecture. About 665. This temple marked the start of radical changes in the layout of temples by incorporating attempts to balance off buildings of different sizes.

24, 25 South side, and columns and stone bases on the north side, Middle Gate, Hōryū-ji, Ikaruga-machi, Ikoma county, Nara prefecture. Length of face of south wall 11.88 m. Late seventh century. The Middle Gate retains what is commonly believed to be the Asuka style of cloud bracketing and exaggerated entasis. Rarely does a Middle Gate have only four bays, which here must be related to the plan of the cloistered area. The base stones for the columns of the main buildings of the Ikaruga-dera were transferred for use when the Hōryū-ji was built some time after 670. Typically variable in size, some unusually flat, these immense stones are the most extraordinary base stones associated with the style of the Asuka period.

5, 27 South and west sides of Main Hall, and model of Main Hall as it appeared until around 710, kept in the Lecture Hall, Hōryū-ji, Ikaruga-machi, Ikoma county, Nara prefecture. Main Hall burned in 1949; rebuilt. The Main Hall houses the Shaka triad, Yakushi statue and Four Heavenly Kings of the Asuka period, and its wall panels carried the celebrated paintings. Typical of early main halls, it is almost square in shape (5 by 4 bays); the upper level is 4 by 3 bays. The porch on the lower level was added in about 710. See *Fig.* 40.

28 Dream Hall (Yumedono), Tō-in, Hōryū-ji, Ikaruga-machi, Ikoma county, Nara prefecture. Height 12.8 m. 739. Named after a building said to have been here, in which Prince Shōtoku received answers in dreams to difficult questions in the scriptures, this is the central building of the eastern part of this temple. Such octagonal buildings have a special memorial significance.

29 Pounded earth and plastered wall, on the north side of the avenue connecting the Tō-in with the Sai-in, Hōryū-ji, Ikaruga-machi, Ikoma county, Nara prefecture. Height about 2.5 m. Several ways of constructing walls were used, but the Chinese technique of pounding layers of earth is one of the oldest and most durable.

30 Gilt bronze statue of Yakushi, Main Hall, Hōryū-ji, Ikaruga-machi, Ikoma county, Nara prefecture. Height 63 cm. Dated by inscription to 607. The statue of the Buddha Yakushi was the chief image for the Hōryū-ji for over a century. The inscription on the

back of the halo gives a date for the founding of the Ikaruga-dera, the first Hōryū-ji.

31 Gilt bronze Shaka triad, Main Hall, Hōryū-ji, Ikaruga-machi, Ikoma county, Nara prefecture. Height of Shaka 87.5 cm. Dated by inscription to 623. A long inscription on the back of the mandorla is the documentation for this group of statues and gives the details concerning Prince Shōtoku's death.

32 North and east sides of five-storeyed pagoda, Hōryū-ji, Ikaruga-machi, Ikoma county, Nara prefecture. Height 32.56 m. Late seventh century. The pagoda had been dismantled when the Main Hall was destroyed by fire in 1949, thus escaping the same fate. The porch on the first floor is an addition of around 710. The first floor had wall paintings, and now has four groups of clay statuettes illustrating events associated with Shaka.

33, 34 Three-storeyed pagoda of Hokki-ji (also called Ikejiri-dera and Okamoto-dera), Okamoto, Ikaruga-machi, Ikoma county, Nara prefecture. Height 23.95 m. 685–706. The pagoda is the only old building that now stands of a small temple which was traditionally founded in 638, but was apparently rebuilt after 685 and finished around 706. It is also the only three-storeyed pagoda of the Asuka style in existence.

35, 36 Three-storeyed pagoda of Yakushi-ji, Nishinokyō, Nara city (jurisdictional area), Nara prefecture. Height 34.14 m. Early eighth century. Although erected on the spot after the beginning of the Nara period, this is the only building standing today which represents the Late Asuka style in its 'proto-Nara' structural system. All of the buildings at this temple had extra roofs inserted between storeys and, in some cases, porches.

37 North side of three-storeyed west pagoda, Taima-dera, Taima village, Kita-katsuragi county, Nara prefecture. Height 24.8 m. Eighth or ninth century. The Taima-dera is the only temple remaining today that retains two pagodas from the time when the twin, axially-arranged pagodas were in style in the late seventh to the middle of the eighth centuries. Unlike the east pagoda here, in which was employed the older method of reducing the number of bays in higher storeys, this one has three on all levels.

38 Stone bases for columns of Main Hall, Hon-yakushi-ji, Kidono, Kashiwara city (jurisdictional area), Nara prefecture. Late seventh century. The site of the early Yakushi-ji, a temple started by Emperor Temmu, is preserved in the form of base stones for the Main Hall and east pagoda, and the base stone for the centre pole of the west pagoda.

39 Stone bases for columns of east pagoda, Hon-yakushi-ji, Kidono, Kashiwara city (jurisdictional area), Nara prefecture. Late seventh century. Most of the shaped stones are intact here for the usual 3 by 3 bay pagoda. The large centre stone held the relics of the temple and was covered by a circular stone laid on the lowest step.

40 Centre pole stone base for the west pagoda, Yakushi-ji, Nishinokyo, Nara city (jurisdictional area). Early eighth century. The pagoda was destroyed in the sixteenth century. This one held the temple's relics when the buildings were moved to Heijō in the early eighth century; the east pagoda held them at the original temple. Of the usual seventeen base stones required to support a pagoda, all but four are still *in situ* for this building. Except for the centre stone, only

two, at the north-east and south-east corners, have been squared off on top. All of the others are natural and appear to have been unworked.

41 Stone base for centre pole of pagoda of Tachibana-dera, Asuka village, Takechi county, Nara prefecture. Diameter of centre of hole 90 cm.; depth of hole 8 cm. Early seventh century. Tradition says Prince Shōtoku founded this temple around 606. It has a unique orientation (see *Fig.* 39). Tiles of the Asuka, Hakuhō, Nara, Heian, Kamakura and Muromachi (1333–1573) periods found here show that the temple was kept in good repair until about the sixteenth century.

42, 43 South side and view from north-east of Main Hall, Tōshōdai-ji, Gojō-machi, Nara city (jurisdictional area). Length of face of south side 28 m. Late eighth century. The 7 by 4 bay building is twice as long as it is deep (96 by 48 ft), and has columns set to provide wider spaces toward the centre of the south and north sides. The chief statues are framed in the three doors. The south bay stands open like a porch.

44 Bronze statues of Yakushi, Nikkō and Gakkō in Main Hall, Yakushi-ji, Nishi-nokyō, Nara city (jurisdictional area). Height of Yakushi 4.10 m.; bodhisattvas each 3.68 m. *c.* 696. These remarkable bronze figures, a reflection of the newly introduced T'ang dynasty style, were once gilded but retain only traces of the gilding today, the over-coating or loss of it the result of several fires. Yakushi is the Buddha of healing. Nikkō, the bodhisattva of the sun, stands on his left; Gakkō, the bodhisattva of the moon, stands on his right; each holds up the inside hand.

45 Bronze head, Treasure Hall, Kōfuku-ji, Nara city. Height 42 cm. 685. Probably a Yakushi, this head is all that remains of a large triad that was once the main image of the Lecture Hall of the Yamada-dera, made between the years 678 and 685. The group was stolen by monks of the Kōfuku-ji in 1184 and installed in that temple's East Main Hall, but the hall was burned by fire resulting from a lightning strike in 1411, destroying most of the statue except the front of the head. At some later time it was deposited under the Buddha platform, and found there in 1937.

46 Clay statue of Miroku, Main Hall, Taima-dera, Taima village, Kita-katsuragi county, Nara prefecture. Height 2.02 m. c. 686. Miroku (Maitreya) was the Buddha of the Future; such a monumental figure may have been related to the recent introduction of the Hossō sect, which paid special regard to Miroku. The right hand gives the sign of abolishing fear. 681 is frequently given for the date of the image, but a date in the neighbourhood of 686 when the temple was almost finished would seem to be the most appropriate.

47 Interior of Main Hall, Tōshōdai-ji, Gojō-machi, Nara city (jurisdictional area). Height of central Buddha 3.03 m. All statues date from the second half of the eighth century. The central image is a dry lacquer Rushana or Birushana (Vairocana), the Universal Buddha which enjoyed considerable popularity throughout east Asia in the eighth century. To his right is a dry lacquer statue of a 1,000-armed Kannon and to his left a Yakushi Buddha. In front, to his right is Bonten and to his left is Taishaku, the Indian deities Brahma and Indra re-spectively. The Four Heavenly Kings stand at the four corners of the platform.

48 South side of Lecture Hall, Tōshōdai-ji, Gojō-machi, Nara city (jurisdictional area). Length of face of wall 33.8 m. 748. Empress Kōken donated this Imperial Assembly Hall from the Heijō Palace c. 754 for the start of this temple, and it was reconstructed to serve as a Lecture Hall in 759–760 by one of the Chinese priests with Ganjin. It is a 9 by 4 bay, rather shallow building (114 ft by 46) with pounded earth floor, in a simple structural style.

49 Wooden storehouse, Tōshōdai-ji, Gojō-machi, Nara city (jurisdictional area). Eighth century. The Tōshōdai-ji has two square, windowless, wooden storage build-ings on the east side of the compound, the slightly smaller of the two being the sūtra repository. The other is shown here. The storehouse type is better known through the Shōsōin in the grounds of the Tōdai-ji.

50 East side of Main Hall (Hondō), Shin-yakushi-ji, Takahata-chō, Nara city. Length of face of wall 22.7 m. Late eighth century. The Shin-yakushi-ji (New Yakushi temple) was built by Empress Kōmyō as a dedication to the Buddha of healing when Emperor Shōmu was ill. The buildings were erected after 747, the temple constructed on a colossal scale. This is the only original structure left and, though now serving as the chief hall of the temple, was only a secondary building in the eighth century, perhaps the refectory. It is, however, informative regard-ing the appearance of side buildings at that time. 7 by 5 bays, with low roof and simple structural details, the interior has no false ceilings and allows the entire structural scheme to be seen.

51 West side of Tegai-mon, Tōdai-ji, Nara city. Length of face of wall 16.6 m. Middle eighth century. The Tegai Gate is the only original one remaining of this vast temple. It was in the north-west of the surrounding wall (see *Fig. 50*).

52 Site of pagoda of Gankō-ji, Shibashinya-chō, Nara city. Length of sides of pagoda on ground floor 10.3 m.; diameter of rounded step of base stone for centre pole 140 cm. Late eighth century. This perfectly preserved site is the only part of this temple's location that can now be seen. The pagoda stood to the east of the main cloistered part of the temple. It consisted of 5 storeys and probably stood about 52 m. high.

53 Round eave-end roof tile, Asuka-dera, Asuka village, Takechi county, Nara prefecture. Diameter 15.1 cm. *c.* 596. National Museum, Tokyo. The Asuka-dera seems to have been the first temple to have had roof tiles, and to have given its name to this type. Initially from Kudara (Paekche), examples are found at sites of a number of Asuka period temples, such as the Ikaruga-dera, Shitennō-ji, Kataokaō-ji, Yokoihai-ji and others. They have nine or ten petals and no surrounding decoration.

54 Square rafter-end tile, Myōon-ji, Toyonaka-chō, Mitoyo county, Kagawa prefecture. 15 by 15 cm. Early seventh century. The tile was nailed by the centre hole to the end of a rafter or a beam. It is essentially a local variation of the Yamada-dera type, of the Late Asuka period. Yamada-dera type tiles are found from the Kantō to Kyushu, in a wide distribution.

55 Section of scroll of the Life of Ippen Shōnin, a priest who lived from 1239–1289 and founded the Ji sect; painted in 1299, by Eni,

.showing the tomb of Prince Shōtoku. As Eni is known to have been a keen observer, this is probably a reasonably accurate representation.

56 Pantile, Yakushi-ji, Nishinokyō, Nara city (jurisdictional area). Late seventh century. National Museum, Tokyo. The ornamental tiles that fit between the round tiles at the ends of the eaves began to appear regularly around the middle of the seventh century. The example here belongs to the Fujiwara Palace type, where tiles seem to have first been used on palace buildings after 694. This one features a top row of beads, a vine pattern, and a bottom row of zigzags.

57 Round eave-end roof tile, Izumo Provincial Temple, Takeya-chō, Matsue city, Shimane prefecture. Diameter 14.5 cm. Mid eighth century. National Museum, Tokyo. This very beautiful tile is quite atypical, having no special counterpart in the Kinki region or elsewhere. It was locally made for the temple which Emperor Shōmu ordered each province to construct. With a very small centre circle for an eighth century tile, the receptacle is surrounded by 7 small but broad petals, a vine pattern and a string of beads that should total 34 in number, all in relatively low relief.

58 Round eave-end roof tile, Daikandai-ji, Asuka village, Takechi county, Nara prefecture. Diameter 21.0 cm. Late seventh century. National Museum, Tokyo. Representative of the so-called Daikandai-ji type, these tiles are commensurate in size with large buildings.

59, 60 Exterior and interior of Iwayayama Tomb, Kashiwara city (jurisdictional area), Nara prefecture. Width of opening at entrance 2.23 m.; length of passageway 5.70 m.;

length of chamber 5.0 m.; width of wall at back 2.78 m. Length of sarcophagus 2.33 m.; width of sarcophagus 1.12 m. Seventh century. An example of the late corridor tombs, much of its entranceway is now exposed. It is generally believed that the interior of Prince Shōtoku's tomb more or less resembles this one.

61 Skeletons in Tunnel tomb 2, Jindai-ji, Mitaka city, (greater) Tokyo. Eighth or ninth century. Three tombs were found in 1962 when a sewer line was being laid, all containing skeletons, in this case a male, a female, and the much decayed bones of a child, lying on a stone floor. Grave goods included a pottery vase of the Sue type and some fragments of ash-glazed pottery.

62 Pottery vase of the traditional Sue type, found in the passageway of Tomb 4, Ōsawa, Mitaka city, (greater) Tokyo. Height 26.0 cm. Ninth or tenth century. International Christian University Collection. A typical, grey, vase-shaped vessel, with blackened areas, of a type known since the late fifth century in Japan; the type was continued with minor variations for several centuries at different centres.

63 Tunnel tombs 2 and 3 (*yokoana* or sideways cave), cut through and partially filled, Ōsawa, Mitaka city, (greater) Tokyo. The openings are 6.8 m. apart. Ninth or tenth century. Scores of these tombs were dug into a loamy bluff that runs through the city of Mitaka and extends for many kilometres on either side, in the western suburbs of metropolitan Tokyo. (See *Fig. 58*).

64 Tomb of Emperor Temmu (d. 686) and Empress Jitō (d. 703), the so-called Hino-kuma Ōuchi Ryō, Asuka village, Takechi county, Nara prefecture. View looking north-west. The top of a hill was cut down to form an eight-sided mound above a square base, in a rare form for the tumuli of the time.

65 Stone stūpa-like structure, called Kuma-yama *kaidan* (meaning a ceremonial platform or stage), Kumayama-chō, Okayama prefecture. Length at base about 7.8 m. on each side; height about 3.7 m. Eighth century. This remote structure is constructed of piled up stones, some roughly shaped, in three stages. A clay tube stood in a central hole and probably served as a container for the ashes of priests (see *Fig. 66*).

66 Gilt bronze cinerary urn for the ashes of Ina no Mabito Ōmura, excavated at Ana-mushiyama, Koshiba-chō, Kita-katsuragi county, Nara prefecture. Height 23.5 cm.; diameter 24.3 cm. 707. Shitennō-ji, Osaka. On the lid of the urn is an inscription in radial lines, giving the details of the man's life.

67, 68 Bronze epitaph box and bronze epitaph of Fumi no Nemaro, excavated at Yataki Kasayama, Uchimaki village, Haibara-chō, Uda county, Nara prefecture. Length of box 29.0 cm.; epitaph 26.1 cm. 707. National Museum, Tokyo. The ashes of this man, who is well documented in the ancient records as a successful general in the Jinshin Revolt of 672 which put Temmu on the throne, were found in 1831 in a cloth-wrapped green glass vessel, which was inside a gilt bronze urn that had apparently been tied with a cord. The epitaph was wound in cloth and laid in the bronze box. It bears two columns of writing in 18 and 17 characters.

69 Relics excavated from the stone base for the centre pole of the pagoda, Sūfuku-ji,

Early Buddhist Japan

Shigasato-chō, Ōtsu city, Shiga prefecture. Length of gilt bronze outer box 10.8 cm. Probably c. 667. Ōmi Shrine, Ōtsu city. This hillside temple now consists only of the foundations of several buildings. The 1938–39 excavations were responsible for the recovery of the relics from a hole on the east side of the stone base of the pagoda's centre pole. They were in a bronze box, successively enclosing silver and gold boxes and a glass jar. Also included were silver coins, a bronze mirror, small bells and beads. (See *Fig.* 1).

70 Back of bronze mirror with Lion and Grape decoration, kept in the Main Hall, Hōryū-ji, Ikaruga-machi, Ikoma county, Nara prefecture. Diameter 23.5 cm. Chinese, late seventh or early eighth century. A so-called 'white copper' mirror, named because of its silvery finish, this large example is probably a fairly early product of a type which enjoyed considerable popularity in the early T'ang period. This may be presumed to be Chinese in make, but many mirrors were produced in Japan into the eighth century with Chinese characteristics. Temples acquired great numbers of mirrors, whether Chinese or Japanese in origin. The property lists for the Daian-ji include 1,275 mirrors for that temple.

71 Three-storeyed stone pagoda, Ishidō-ji, Gamō-chō, Shiga prefecture. Height 4.64 m. Late seventh century. A group of Koreans are recorded as arriving in Japan and being given a place to settle in this area in 669. This pagoda is doubtless their work. Built of large slabs of granite, a small squarish hole was cut in the south side of the third stage to act as a relic repository.

72 Thirteen-storeyed rock-cut stone pagoda, Rokutani-ji, Taishi-chō, Osaka prefecture.

Height 5.28 m. Late seventh century. The crest of a tufa hill was cut away to produce this pagoda, a grotto and some high relief, now very badly weathered, figures. The group lies about 1.3 km. from the top of Mt Nijō on the Osaka side. One hole for relics was cut into the pagoda just below the first stage on the south side, and another one can be seen above the fourth storey on the east side. The cap is missing.

73 Some of the miniature wooden pagodas in the Hōryū-ji, Ikaruga-machi, Ikoma county, Nara prefecture. Height of largest about 45 cm. Probably 764. These must be part of the donation presented by Empress Shōtoku around 764 to several temples: the Hōryū-ji still has thousands. They are made of Japanese cypress (*hinoki*) on a kind of lathe, and are mostly painted white, but occasionally either in red, green or yellow.

74 Stone bearing two faces in relief (on either end), in the grounds of the Tachibana-dera, Asuka village, Takechi county, Nara prefecture. Height 1.15 m.; thickness 62.5 cm. Late sixth or early seventh century. This granitic stone is now on the spot where the Lecture Hall of the Tachibana-dera once stood. The two-faced idea may be related to the *dōso-jin*, the road guardians, where two figures are often juxtaposed.

75, 77 Monkey Stones (*Saruishi*), two stone figures placed in front of Hinokuma tomb, near Tachibana-dera train station, Asuka village, Takechi county, Nara prefecture. Height of 75, 82.7 cm.; 77, 72 cm. These weather-worn figures have been moved out of fields (according to existing records) and were finally deposited in front of this small circular tomb attributed to the wife of a descendant of Emperor Bidatsu, which lies to the west of the large keyhole-shaped mound of Emperor Kimmei.

76 Monkey Stone (*Saruishi*), now at Takatori Castle, Takatori-chō, Nara prefecture. Height 80 cm. Late sixth or early seventh century. Said to have been found near the tomb of Emperor Kimmei.

78 Stone Shumisen (Mt Sumeru), an object now standing in the grounds of the National Museum, Tokyo, from Asuka, Asuka village, Takechi county, Nara prefecture. Height 2.34 m. Probably 657. Three separate pieces of granite form a hollow base, a central ring and a cap, decorated with reliefs of undulating mountains; together they presumably symbolize the Buddhist holy mountain.

79 So-called *Dōso-jin* or Roadside Protective Deity, a stone statue now standing in the grounds of the National Museum, Tokyo, from Ishigami, Asuka village, Takechi county, Nara prefecture. Height 1.74 m. Late sixth or early seventh century. It seems to represent joined male and female figures and is perhaps a prototype of the kind of statue still occasionally seen along roads in some parts of Japan.

80 Masuda Iwafune, Minami-miyohōji hill, Kashiwara city (jurisdictional area), Nara prefecture. Length of worked area on top about 7.50 m.; width of top level surface at middle about 3.82 m. A large, natural outcrop of stone was smoothed and cut into, providing it with two holes each about 1.60 by 1.50 m., with a depth of over 1.50, but with sloping floors. View looking north-east.

81 Oni no Setchin (Demon's toilet), at Kirigamine, Asuka village, Takechi county, Nara prefecture. Length 3.90 m.; width

3.15 m. Late sixth or early seventh century. Local tradition to the contrary, this is probably the body of a large stone sarcophagus, the lid perhaps the flat slab that lies on the hillside above it, just across the road (Plate 83). A hole at one end that could be sealed with a door is not uncommon in Late Tomb period sarcophagi.

82 Turtle Stone (*Kameishi*), at Kawahara, Asuka village, Takechi county, Nara prefecture. Length 4.20 m.; width 2.80 m.; exposed height 2.05 m. Late sixth or early seventh century. The granite stone lies in a field about 500 m. south-west of the Tachibana-dera. Its south-west side is shaped to resemble an eyebrow line and eyes, another side resembles a leg.

83 Oni no Manaita (Demon's chopping board), at Kirigamine, Asuka village, Takechi county, Nara prefecture. Length 4.37 m.; maximum width 2.90 m.; exposed thickness 75 cm. Late sixth or early seventh century. It is possible that this large slab was the lid of the box-shaped stone object shown in Plate 81.

84 *Sakafune-ishi* (Rice-wine-boat stone), above Oka-dera on the hillside, Asuka village, Takechi county, Nara prefecture. Length 5.45 m.; maximum width 2.30 m.; exposed height at middle 1.03 m. Late sixth to early seventh century. Shallow basins and shallower drains give the impression that the stone was used for a brewing process or the production of oil. The latter is more likely.

85 Standing stone in the grounds of the Asuka Niimasu Shrine, Asuka village, Takechi county, Nara prefecture. Height about 1.40 m. Date uncertain. An avenue of approach zigzagging up the hill lined with stones of phallic shape is supplemented with open

terraces on higher levels at this shrine. Large stones, as illustrated here, are situated on these terraces, the plot surrounded by straw rope and the largest stone itself draped in the same way to recognize its sanctity.

86 Stone relief of Shaka triad, Ishii-dera, Osaka, Sakurai city (jurisdictional area), Nara prefecture. Height 1.14 m.; width 1.18 m.; thickness at base 30 cm. Early eighth century. Sometimes claimed to be the oldest stone Buddhist triad in Japan, this sandstone sculpture is in perfect condition, even bearing a little of what must be the original red paint on the lips and drapery of the right side figure. Since stone carvings of this type were intended for exterior use,

this particular one must have been moved inside many centuries ago.

87, 88 Two of the thirteen stones bearing reliefs of Buddhist figures, memorial mound called Zutō, Kami-shimizu-chō, Nara city. Length of each stone about 1.5 m. Probably *c.* 767. Plate 87 shows a simple triad with a Buddha making the hand gestures common to Shaka, the Buddha of this world, and Plate 88 illustrates a more complex group, with seated bodhisattvas and four other haloed figures before a temple building, with a Buddha making gestures typical of both Shaka and Yakushi, yet the grouping as a whole is not unlike the eighth century paradises of Amida. (See *Fig. 67*).

Index

Index

Index